Tim Gunn

A GUIDE TO
QUALITY, TASTE & STYLE

Tim Gunn

A GUIDE TO
QUALITY, TASTE & STYLE

with
Kate Moloney

ABRAMS IMAGE
NEW YORK

Library of Congress Cataloging-in-Publication Data:

Gunn, Tim.
Tim Gunn : a guide to quality, taste, and style / by Tim Gunn with
Kate Moloney.
p. cm.
ISBN: 978-0-8109-9284-9 (hardcover with jacket)
1. Clothing and dress. 2. Fashion. I. Moloney, Kate. II. Title.

TT507.G86 2007
646'.34—dc22
2007003860

Illustrations by Lainé Roundy
Designer: Becky Terhune
Editors: Tamar Brazis and Susan Van Metre

Printed and bound in U.S.A.
10 9 8 7 6 5 4

Abrams Image books are available at special discounts when purchased in
quantity for premiums and promotions as well as fundraising or educational use.
Special editions can also be created to specification.
For details, contact specialmarkets@abramsbooks.com or the address below.

THE ART OF BOOKS SINCE 1949
115 West 18th Street
New York, NY 10011
www.abramsbooks.com

We dedicate this book to all those who aspire to quality,
taste, and style, and to those who have achieved it!
—T.G. and K.M.

Contents

Tim Gunn

A GUIDE TO
QUALITY, TASTE & STYLE

Chapter One

Who You Are

The Lesson: Understanding and acknowledging who you are is the most important key to the content of your wardrobe. If you consider your wardrobe to be a sphinx, then the sphinx's riddle is surely, "who are you?" Only you possess the answer. Who you are can take us down the longest metaphysical road, so try not to get swept up in too much brooding self-examination and analysis. This doesn't have to be daunting. In fact, we believe this book can make it fun.

"Know, first, who you are;
and then adorn yourself accordingly."
—Epictetus

from the desk
of
TIM GUNN

A NOTE BEFORE WE BEGIN

Dressed in white slacks and an off-the-shoulder sweater, Diane von Furstenberg uses an asparagus spear to tidy the couscous left on her lunch plate. We're sitting amidst Moroccan serving platters of marinated chicken and green salad at the gorgeous and exotic dining table in her enormous loft in the far West Village. She looks up at me and declares, "Tim, you must never lose your voice as an educator." That was her response when I first told her about this book, and it has resonated in me during each and every day of writing. Diane is a dear friend and colleague, and a huge supporter of design education. She is a wise counsel, an oracle, and I adore her for her always frank conversations and occasional outbursts of tough love.

This book is not intended to be an oracle, but it is intended to offer wise counsel and, I hope, inspiration. The centerpiece of the book is you, the reader. I ask that you rid yourself of boundaries and barriers in order to truthfully examine who you are and what your lifestyle is like with the same directness and tough love that Diane von Furstenberg extended to me. This book doesn't want to change you. You are who you are for a reason. I want the content of this book to enhance you, accentuating your positive aspects and mitigating your negative ones.

Unlike the designers I work with on television and my students at Parsons, you and I are not face to face. So don't harbor any concerns that I'm going to stare you down with shock or incredulity. I'll let *you* do that! The goal of this book is to provide you with the tools for an honest self-analysis. I want you to have an epiphany; that is, a moment when reading or reflecting that causes you to emit, "Eureka! I get it!" After your self-awareness is honed, then any actions in response to your epiphany are owned by you.

QUALITY, TASTE & STYLE

"Quality, Taste, and Style," is my operative tenet for most of what I do. It's another way of saying, "The Best." I aim to achieve that in everything from my work at Parsons to my critiques of the designers on television to fixing a meal or cleaning my apartment. Why take on an endeavor if you're not committed to doing your best? I hope to inspire you to better understand your own standards for quality, taste, and style, as defined by you.

None of this is easy. It requires commitment and discipline. While writing, I was constantly examining myself and took both pain and pleasure when putting to practice my own advice. Just this morning, I found myself presented with a clothing dilemma. In preparation for a ten-day trip, I had several suits and many shirts at the dry cleaner that wouldn't be ready for another day. A heavy wool suit loomed at me, but it was inappropriate for this unseasonably warm late-October day. My black suits struck me as being too dressy for those with whom I would engage, so separates—pants, sportcoats—seemed to be the answer. It struck me that a closet isn't a clothing store. It's a collection of items that reside there for the purpose of being chosen—or not. So why is it that I so frequently ponder and search, but come up empty, declaring, "I'll need to shop for X so that this dilemma can be reconciled"? That's the wrong approach. The correct approach is to make it work! I merely need to take my own medicine!

MAKE IT WORK!

"Make it work!" is an enormously useful expression. I remember the first time I used it. It was roughly six years ago in one of my classes at Parsons. I find that often students who struggle with an assignment are inclined to abandon the struggle and begin again. This practice unnerves me, because it's like playing roulette with one's work. What assurance does one have that the next spin of the wheel will be successful? Important learning occurs when a struggle is examined and analyzed, diagnosed, and a prescription offered. Ergo, make it work. I believe that we all benefit from the make-it-work practice.

So I suggest that we all come to terms with what fashion looks we gravitate toward and then analyze them for their particulars: items of apparel, color stories, accessories, even hair and makeup. Think of this process as being like playing with Colorforms. The items of apparel and accessories are discreet components designed to be mixed and matched. You're selecting and placing them on an image of you, so take into account your coloring, your height, and your silhouette. Look carefully at the proportion of the clothes in relation to your body and the proportions of each item in relation to the others. Where does the skirt's hem end on your leg? What about the jacket's shoulders and arm length? Where does the jacket hit the skirt? With each and every addition of an item, silhouette and proportion change. Be attentive to these myriad moving parts! Start asking these questions and more: Which fabrics do you feel most comfortable in? How do you accessorize? Where do you shop? What does your carriage say about you?

MILIEU AND ITS ATTENDANT EXPECTATIONS

Notice that this chapter is not titled "Who Are You?" That question strikes me as being quasi-confrontational. I'm reminded of the chilling scene in *The Wizard of Oz* when Dorothy, the Scarecrow, the Tin Man, and the Cowardly Lion stand before a stage of fire and brimstone, replete with voluminous clouds of spewing smoke. An apparition, the hydrocephalic emerald green Wizard, bellows at them, "Who are you?!" in a manner that challenges their mere existence. I love the fact that you exist!

Who you are embraces everything about you, from your family's origins to your predilections for particular films and music, to your fantasies and reveries, to your weekly routines. It's also your size, shape, and proportions, and your coloring. And it's the city or town in which you live, your home, and your friends and colleagues. It's milieu.

With milieu comes attendant expectations. How we dress sends a message about who we are, or at least how we want the world to perceive us. It's the semiology of clothes. Although I'm not a fan of Roland Barthes, I do subscribe to his theory that language is a self-contained system of signs. How we dress is a personal form of language; it is highly informed by our society and culture. So, as you face your wardrobe and prepare to dress for the day, project yourself onto a billboard in Times Square. How will people respond to that image of you, and what assumptions will they make about who you are?

While I acknowledge that who I am is a synthesis of my genetic makeup, my upbringing, my education, and my life experience, when I seriously home in on the essence of me, it's my professional life that defines me. Although a New Yorker for close to a quarter of a century, my sartorial roots are in Washington, D.C.

I love my hometown, but let's be honest, with the exception of the dazzling Kennedy years, Washington is a fashion desert. When I was younger, Brooks Brothers was my haberdasher of choice, and while I respect its market, it's hardly fashion forward. As a struggling sculptor in D.C., I survived by building architectural models and had a wardrobe of jeans, khakis, and T-shirts, which was appropriate enough. Later, I began teaching three-dimensional design at the Corcoran, so I paired the jeans and khakis with button-down oxford shirts. When I began working in the Corcoran's Office of Admissions, I traveled nationwide to recruit students, so I added neckties and a navy blazer to my wardrobe. Later still, with more maturity and responsibility, I added suits—my favorite at that time being a gray glen plaid. When I accepted a position at Parsons and moved to New York in 1983, the D.C. wardrobe followed. I wore it with no regard for the fashion circus that is New York. I wasn't out of place, because you can wear anything in the City That Never Sleeps, but I wasn't acknowledging the expanded possibilities that the city provided for my wardrobe, either. But, eventually, I did add Ralph Lauren to my vocabulary, partially because their flagship at 72nd Street and Madison Avenue is one of the most spectacular interiors on earth. Who wouldn't want to visit?!

For years and years, I was Associate Dean at Parsons. In that capacity, I wore a suit and tie every day—gray, grayer, and grayest. Frankly, it wasn't until my position at Parsons shifted to Chair of the Department of Fashion Design—temporarily I thought—that I came to sobering terms with who I am. It was sobering, indeed, to look at myself objectively and see a stuffy, buttoned-up old fart. I became very aware of Donna Karan's glares, Marc Jacobs's snickers, and Diane von Furstenberg's slight sniffs of disdain. Whether the position was temporary or not, I needed to be modernized. Still, I hesitated. But when I received a permanent appointment a year later. . . I went shopping! My goal was to find a black leather blazer. Why? Because it's hip and therefore modern, yet the soul of the blazer is, by definition, conservative.

Look, I am only too cognizant of the fact that I am not a Dolce & Gabbana or Dsquared2 kind of guy, so a leather blazer was an excellent transitional piece for me. I found a great one at Saks. It was Hugo Boss and it was —gulp—$800. I loved it. I bought it. And I left Saks in a retail daze, because $800 was my clothing budget for the year. I crossed Fifth Avenue to Rockefeller Center and stumbled into Banana Republic. I recognized that I was in a stupor, but I believed that I spotted a black leather blazer identical to the one I just bought. Was that possible? I moved forward and, sure enough, it was entirely possible. More important, the blazer was only $400! I bought it. I even opened a Banana Republic account and saved 20 percent, too. Then, I crossed Fifth Avenue, again, to return the earlier purchase. I was so proud of myself: mission accomplished and at a 50 percent savings! Most notable for me was that with that blazer, I experienced for the first time and first-hand the incredible virtues of black: It's sophisticated, slimming, and always in style. Furthermore, you don't have to think about "does this go with that?" It's black. It goes. So now I have a closet filled with black suits, black jackets, black shirts, black sweaters, and black shoes. I can't go back from black!

I'm not advocating that you wear the same thing in the same color day after day, but most of us are comfortable with a uniform. By "uniform," I don't mean a Stepford Wife blueprint of exacting sameness. I mean a cache of categories of separates that can successfully interact. My mother is constantly asking me how it can be that I wear so much black, adding, "And how many black turtlenecks must you own?" I know what I'm confident wearing, because I know that these articles of apparel look good on me. I'd say that I have five or six looks and iterations thereof. This makes selecting a look for the day a fairly easy exercise for me. I look at my itinerary, see which appointments I have and with whom, and dress for the highest level of expectation for that day.

I believe that most of us think the same way about our wardrobe; that is, we *like* having a uniform. Not one uniform, but a number of various looks, the components of which can be mixed around and accessorized. It's essential that you identify looks—not merely items of clothing, but combinations that will be worn together: the silhouettes, proportions, colors, and textures of which flatter and enhance you. Then, stick with them! Do not stray! And don't ever forget about fit!

Never forget that fashion, *your* fashion, cannot be comprehensively assessed without projecting it onto you; you need to try clothes on and look at yourself (and I prefer a three-way mirror for this purpose). When speaking about fashion and proportion, proportion includes the relationship between the clothes and your body; that is, what proportion is created between the hem of your skirt and your footwear, the bust-line of your dress and your neck and shoulders? If you observe these matters and can make the proportions work (and there's no reason why any one of us can't), then you're light years ahead of the pack.

As you look in that three-way mirror, there are some questions to ponder, some traps to avoid. But before we describe these traps, we want to talk about vocabulary—the words and phrases you need to ask yourself the right questions about your style choices.

HELPFUL WORDS AND PHRASES

I subscribe to the notion of "Learn the grammar, then add the vocabulary." Most people would attribute that statement to learning a foreign language. Indeed, fashion can be a foreign language. I am mindful of the power of vocabulary; it can unleash limitless quantities of defining and descriptive words and phrases that awaken the listener or the reader to new dimensions of understanding. (Whew! That sounds overly grand, doesn't it?) But vocabulary can derail, render impotent, and befuddle meanings or intended meanings. The words that we choose to critically analyze people, places, and things are especially important, and we must be responsibly cognizant of what we intend to say.

Let's take a fashion critique as an example, because I deal with this topic day in and day out. I ask my students to please not use the phrases, "I like it," and "I don't like it," because, frankly, who cares whether you like it or don't like it? Allow yourself to make a distinction between what appeals to you and what works for you. (If you love chartreuse but it looks dreadful on you, get your chartreuse fix around the house: perhaps some throw pillows would do it.) The critique should be about the qualities and/or inadequacies of what you see. Although everything we observe we see through a lens that is informed by our experiences, I must insist that you not personalize what you see.

Although we (you and I) are, indeed, shopping together, metaphorically that is, I caution my students to *not* shop when looking critically at fashion. I advise my colleagues similarly when watching a fashion show. One colleague railed at me after the Annual Parsons Fashion Show last May:

COLLEAGUE:	"That menswear was terrible!"
ME:	"You thought so? Why?"
COLLEAGUE:	"Why? It was awful! I wouldn't wear any of it!"
ME:	"Well, the students didn't design it with you in mind as the customer."
	(And given the colleague, my last remark was an understatement.)

Is it surprising that my colleague had nothing at all to say about the womenswear? No, because he was shopping for himself!

So, let me suggest some opening phrases that can allow you to have a more meaningful exchange of thoughts and observations:

POSITIVE:
"I find this (insert item here) to be compelling, because . . ."
"I respond well to this, because . . ."
"I'm attracted to this, because . . ."

NEGATIVE:

"I'm not responding well to this, because . . ."

"This isn't working for me, because . . ."

When considering things that you respond to, let me add that it's important to express something, anything, even if you think you can't find the correct word or words. If your viscera are saying, "no," then listen.

Let me also suggest that you steer clear of statements that describe things that can't be changed, or are unlikely to change, and matters that don't advance the plot: "My foot is too long" is an example of the former and, "Everything I wear makes me look fat," is an example of the latter.

THE AGE TRAP: BABY JANE VS. THE SCHOOLMARM

The crimes of age and appropriateness are usually in the form of older women trying to look like teenagers. However, I have also witnessed too many cases of younger women dressing like matronly schoolmarms. The latter may be a matter of preference, although the question of "why?" eludes me. The former is simply sad. The only thing sadder is an older man, lifted and tucked, dyed and coiffed, and all dandied out. These Gustav von Aschenbachs make me want to weep.

For some reason, Manhattan's Upper East Side is the *ne plus ultra* incubator for grandma jezebels and teenyboppers. Although surgical and non-surgical forms of cosmetic enhancement can successfully transform a face, I have yet to learn of a procedure that can transform an Egyptian mummy into a wrinkle-free neonate. Just walk down Madison Avenue on a weekday afternoon and you'll see the parade of Nefertitis, some in miniskirts and bandeaus of spandex (plus a mink coat in winter), and others in Parisian couture, usually vintage Lacroix. It's all so horrifying to observe. But we should put these circus sideshows away, because they can't be fixed. It's too late and their commitment to this look is too powerful. Instead, let's look at what can be fixed.

Agnes Gooch, or the dowdy schoolmarm, is a look that makes younger women appear thirty years older. I work with some people in this category: A baggy dirndl is their idea of a party dress. The schoolmarm assumes the look and posture of a sack of potatoes, so it's not just the clothes that label her; it's her carriage, too. You can wear a plaid skirt, a basic white shirt, and a tailored jacket and still look youthful and even a little sexy. Remember our mantra: silhouette, proportion, fit.

THE COMFORT TRAP

Is it just my perception or have we really become a nation of slobs? It's a good thing that my maternal grandmother died in 1982 (she was always impeccable in a suit and hat), because the erosion of wardrobe protocols from the late '80s onward would have destroyed her. It's old news that sweats have become the de rigueur travel ensemble. And sadly, I'm used to LaGuardia Airport looking like a gymnasium—I don't even notice those fleece getups anymore. I merely wish that they were confined to airports and health clubs. Recently, I was at the theater with the divine and always superbly dressed Grace Mirabella, former editor-in-chief of *Vogue* and founder of *Mirabella* magazine. There we were in incomprehensibly expensive orchestra seats, and a couple scoots by us in matching workout suits. We were seeing Vanessa Redgrave in a Eugene O'Neill epic—not Cirque du Soleil. I wanted to shout, "Grace, don't look!" But I was too late.

And then there's the flip-flop phenomenon. Ugh. How is it that these slabs of rubber can proliferate so, even in winter? Where is this taking our society and culture other than into a long and winding fashion decline?

I'm not saying that you need to be trussed and harnessed like a rack of lamb, but consider semiotics: You're sending a message about who you are. I'm perfectly comfortable as I sit and write this, and I'm wearing jeans and a turtleneck. If firefighters were to burst into the room right now, I'd feel presentable. (This scenario is not implausible. It happened to me a number of years ago, when a neighbor thought that she saw smoke coming from one of my windows. It wasn't. And the firefighters couldn't have been more friendly and conciliatory.) But I will confess that I have my own slob ensemble—the world's most comfortable, but wrecked, T-shirts and drawstring workout pants—but it doesn't leave my apartment. And even *I* will troop over to the local deli for coffee, a bagel, and *The New York Times* wearing shorts and flip-flops, providing it's summer. But with very few exceptions, I dress to meet and greet and engage without feeling underdressed or overdressed for the occasion. Listen, I'm not just talking about shopping at Barneys or meeting Diane von Furstenberg for a drink. We engage with someone when we pay for something, so merely leaving your home is a set-up for engagement. Oh, shut up, Tim.

I believe that the concept of "casual Fridays" in the workplace wreaked more havoc on women than men. We know that too many men went beyond the boundaries of good sense, let alone good taste, when golf shirts, madras shorts, and flip-flops began appearing. Thankfully, there ensued a negative response and men stepped back to adjust. Many women, on the other hand, saw this concept as an opportunity to be casual and stay casual. I have nothing at all against the word "casual" and its meaning. But it is not to be conflated with inappropriate attire, such as pajamas at work. With precious few exceptions, the people with whom I work in the Department of Fashion Design are very well-dressed and put together. But I work with a lot of people at the University, too, and the same cannot be said about some of them. I attended a meeting recently at which someone (gender makes no difference in this case) was wearing flannel drawstring pants printed with soccer balls. Even deadpan me couldn't conceal my incredulity! I can't remember what was worn on top. The pants, alone, did me in.

And may I make one request of everyone? Please conceal your midriff. I continue to see far too many people in jeans (usually low-slung) with a little shrunken top that stops about an inch above the belly button. Unless you possess amazing abs and are attending a workout, please, please, please avoid this look at all costs. It's dreadful. And it's dreadful at any age.

THE COSTUME TRAP

I know of some people who use the content of their wardrobe to assemble some of the wackiest getups I've ever seen—and that's quite a statement coming from me. If it were a wacky ensemble that consistently evoked the same message, then that would be one thing, and perhaps even laudable (think Patricia Field or Anna Piaggi). But inconsistent wackiness is what I call "the costume trap." The people I know who belong to this category defend their fashion schizophrenia by stating that they hate being the same person day in and day out, adding that they're just having a little fun. Really? At whose expense? Your own!

Let's invoke semiotics, again. How do you want the world to perceive you? If your answer is, "I don't give a damn," then fine, do what you want to do. But if you're like most of us, you care what people think. If we're confident in how we look and someone chooses to reject our taste, then fine, reject us. We're still confident. I've had people look at me, raise an eyebrow, and sneer. "You look so, uh, starched." Thank you. I *am* starched! If, on the other hand, someone was to comment, "Whatever possessed you to wear a white tuxedo?" I would take serious pause, because I would know that I had a lapse in judgment. The same can be said for any outfit that causes you to check your calendar to see if it's October 31.

I am known to raise an eyebrow at many of the designs shown during the Paris couture season—especially the work of John Galliano. This usually results in some cries of anguish from my students, because many of them revere his work. I maintain that fashion isn't relevant if you can't get into a taxi wearing it, and so many of these Galliano creations couldn't fit into a moving van, let alone a yellow cab. My students retort, "But Galliano's work has a market and a place." I agree, but it's limited. *Chacon à son goût.* On that topic, many fashion editors believed Sofia Coppola's *Marie Antoinette* would trigger a fashion frenzy. Huh? A frenzy for what, panniers? I don't think so. I don't believe that the women of the world want to dress like extras in a costume epic.

Ask yourself, "Am I wearing the clothes or are the clothes wearing me?" If the answer is the latter, then you're in the costume trap.

A NOTE ABOUT KATE MOLONEY

Who's Kate? Kate is a dear friend, a colleague, my Assistant Chair in the Department of Fashion Design at Parsons, and a spiritual partner. She is the only person I know whom I'd trust with the responsibility of partnering in the writing of this book. And I wouldn't have agreed to write it without her. A generation younger than I, Kate embraces the world in a way that I can't even comprehend. She is a perpetual student of society and culture, and is among the few truly well-read people I know. Furthermore, she possesses a fabulous fashion sense. "Quality, Taste, and Style" is Kate!

We hope to challenge you, provoke you, and cause you to question your assumptions. Our goal is for you to be unflinchingly confident in who you are. Own that person. Own your look.

The Blind Spot: Examining "who you are" is not intended to be an opportunity to morph from Agnes Gooch to Barbarella. It's not about shaking your underpinnings or creating a Hyde from a Jekyll. You should consider your transformation to be an enhancement, not a new identity through a sartorial version of the Witness Protection Program.

Chapter Two

The Fit Conundrum

The Lesson: We all strive to have our wardrobe fit us like a glove. Due to our unique proportions and the vagaries of sizing, it sometimes seems the best we'll be able to achieve is finding clothing that fits like a mitten. In this chapter we'll discuss how to best dress a host of body types and why exactly you can wear a size 2 at Banana Republic, while you fit quite nicely into Aunt Elise's vintage 14s. It isn't magic, it isn't the South Beach Diet; in fact, it isn't even important. This chapter is about finding a great fit, not a number on a tag. Read on.

"She wears her clothes as if
they were thrown on her with a pitchfork."
—Jonathan Swift

THE CHALLENGE OF A GOOD FIT

Among the most easily resolved of the fashion foibles is fit. Surely we all agree that pants should not pool around our shoes, nor should jackets keep us from moving our arms. And yet, multitudes wear clothes that are too big or too small. When they ask, "How do I look?" we're much more inclined to respond, "Like a sack of potatoes" or "Like you're wearing a sausage casing."

These people are being done in by fit. Keep in mind that this is not an issue of size, as in *your* size. This is an issue of the size and shape of your garments and whether they work to accentuate "all the things you are." That phrase is cribbed, of course, from Oscar Hammerstein II and Jerome Kern, two men of very different physical proportions—Oscar was tall and robust, Jerome was not—who both managed to look good while writing some truly wonderful songs. Despite the genius of their artistic partnership, Oscar would have looked ridiculous in one of Jerome's suits, and vice versa. Yet every day, the equivalent takes place: Hammersteins wake up and try to wedge themselves in Kern clothes, and the Kerns assume they can roll up the sleeves of that sweater that is too big but was on sale.

Furthermore, some larger Hammersteins—i.e., plus-size women and men—hold on to the mythology that larger-size clothes conceal weight and girth. They don't. They accentuate it. Witness the muumuu, that dress-me-up look from the '70s that was all the rage for cocktail attire from poolside to penthouse. We won't assail its comfort, but it made even petite women look like floats in a parade. Surely the muumuu is just a tattersall away from a housedress (think Shirley Booth in *Come Back, Little Sheba*).

Consider the *ne plus ultra* of plus-size quality, taste, and style, the quintessential diva: the prima donna. We'd place Leontyne Price—all size 24 of her—on a pedestal next to Audrey Hepburn any day. La Price knows what clothing proportions look good with her own proportions, what colors work with her skin tones, and she is aware of the critical importance of fit. In addition, she is aware of the extraordinary benefits of good posture. Audrey Hepburn, physically quite a different type from la Price, did exactly the same thing for her size. Think of all those iconic Audrey images: Her clothing is graphic and has a minimum of fussy detail, the hair swept back or the short, short bangs. Neither woman tried to dress as someone she was not, and both looked fabulous. Size had nothing to do with it.

FASHION'S OC

Fit is the most neglected aspect of how we dress; that is, most people wear clothes that are either too big or too small or a combination of both. Why? In the case of clothes that are too big, we suspect that it's an issue of comfort. One of our tenets is: If your goal when dressing is to feel as though you never got out of bed, then don't.

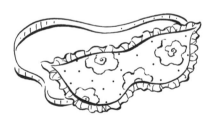

Get out of bed, that is. Pants that drag on the floor, tops that come down to your knees, a coat that hits your ankle, these are items that are entirely too big. Dissenters tell us that they "like the drape" that fuller clothes provide. Really? A top that looks like a pup tent is hardly what we call a flattering drape. Instead, it's sloppy. If you're a member of the Oversize Club (fashion's version of "The OC"), experiment with some clothespins. Pinch the fabric in strategic places in order to play with the fit of the garment. You'll notice that you look neater and trimmer, and you'll achieve a more anthropomorphic shape.*

And there are no fewer falsehoods with apparel that is too small. A stretched, puckered sausage skin is as far from flattering as the dirigible housedress. In fact, it can be visually painful to see a woman bursting from her clothes.

And surely it must be physically painful for the wearer. Let us recount the story of a young college girl who took this problem to the extreme. Everything she wore, including her bra and her shoes, was several sizes too small. "Valerie" would literally limp around campus, and a flight of stairs made her breathless, because she wasn't able to fully use her lungs. A group of classmates performed an intervention. Tearfully, Valerie stated that her confining, suffocating wardrobe made her look smaller and thinner. Preposterous! We never learned the full outcome of the intervention, other than that Valerie found a psychotherapist. Hopefully, she was helped.

WHAT SIZE ARE YOU? OR THE LYING, DECEPTIVE SHELL GAME OF VANITY SIZING

Size is just a construct. However, we are conditioned to think, "Ah, I'm a size 6, so I'm fabulous!" The size label in women's clothes (fortunately, it hasn't struck men . . . yet) is a retail-driven plot to obfuscate the expanding

---

* My mother belongs to the OC (the Oversize Club), and I cannot shake her of this problem. She intractably subscribes to the falsehood that she looks less fat, (as opposed to looking thinner), by wearing XXL. Wrong, Mother.

American girth and to reinforce myths associated with sizes. The outcome is a considerable conundrum: "What size am I?"

Vanity sizing is a contrivance of the retail world—not the design industry. The thinking goes like this: Imagine the potential consequence of the consumer who is confronted with the "truth" about her size; that is, she's not the size 10 she thought she was, but she's actually a size 18. The retail world fears that this consumer will flee from the store empty-handed. Of course, once one realizes how variable these numbers are—and this may take some practice—it will allow you to focus on fit, not size.

Retailers seem to be confident that there are advantages to this ploy, but I don't see any advantages to the consumer. We'd venture a guess that retailers actually lose business because customers don't always have the time to try on the same skirt in four different sizes, so they end up returning what doesn't fit.

Why, then, are there no standardized sizes? In fact, there are (and we teach them at Parsons), but it's very misleading to assert that. Why? Because that statement implies to the consumer that all size 8s, for example, are the same—they're not. Why? Two factors are involved. First, the design of the garment determines the placement of the waist, the sleeve length, the length of the skirt, the diameter of the jacket, etc. These factors are why some clothes are slim-fitted while others are boxy or blouson. The second factor is related to price. For example, why is a Donna Karan Collection basic black dress (about $7,500) in a size 8 an entirely different fit than a DKNY basic black dress (about $350) in the same size? Because sizing has changed at the mid-to-lower end of the price scale and has remained the same for 40 years at the higher end. High-end designer-label clothes have never changed their sizing. Your mother's Oscar de la Renta cocktail dress is the same size 6 today as it was when she bought it twenty-five years ago. (And it's interesting to note that European sizes—high-end to low-end—haven't changed, either, but that's another story.)

So, the DKNY size 8 is really an old-world size 10/12. Take three size 8 dress forms, manufactured in 1984, 1994, and 2004. The difference in the waist measurement alone is a full two inches: 1984—25.5, 1994—26.25, 2004—27.5. Interesting, yes? But rather confusing in the dressing room, no? And all of this is done because retailers fear women won't buy if confronted with a number they don't like.

Perhaps the average shopper might be daunted, but the truly stylish person regards that provocative number on the tag with philosophical detachment. One idea that may help to foster that sense of detachment is the following: Buying off the rack is simply flawed. Sadly, most of us are denied the pleasure of made-to-order garments and must rely on what is available to us in stores, or "on the rack." Even the most perfect physiques, though, cannot always find exactly what they need. Think about it: Our bodies are all so different, yet we expect to fit neatly into one size category. Isn't that rather silly?

If you look great in something, who cares what size it is? In fact, that question could almost become a Zen koan: If the size 8 fits, but makes me look bigger, while the size 10 flows gracefully over my figure, actually making me appear smaller, which size should actually be considered the "larger" size? Finally, if that higher number is truly so loathsome to you, cut the tag out with manicure scissors as soon as you get home.

So, how do you know what size to shop for? Try it on! Unless you're shopping a brand that you wear often and know well, never make any assumptions about the fit. Virtually all mass-market companies (inexpensive to bridge) have bought into the vanity-sizing scheme, because their customer base is broad, widespread, and represents most of America. What to do? While shopping, grab the size you think will fit, as well as one size up and down. You may decide that you prefer the slightly longer length of the size up or the more tailored fit of the size down. You won't know unless you try.

SILHOUETTE AND PROPORTION

Once you conquer the fit conundrum, are you foible free? We're afraid not. We're tempted to sing the praises of the golden mean, the Rosetta stone of form and proportion in the Western World, but its use can be complicated, especially when we're considering a multitude of moving parts. Your body has form and proportion, each of your body parts has form and proportion, and each article of your attire has form and proportion. They must all be examined and assessed together!

In the absence of a set of customized paper dolls (isn't that a great idea?), let's conjure which silhouettes and proportions you should embrace and which you should avoid. And we make an assumption about a shared goal of most readers; that is, to find proportions and silhouettes that together make your body look as long and lean as possible under the circumstances.

So, find yourself among the body types on the following pages. More than one category will be true for most people, so mix and match where appropriate. Perhaps you are short-waisted and busty, or petite and short-waisted. Fear not! Although we all have parts of us that we don't like, there is absolutely no reason that thick calves or a concave chest should stand between you and your style goals. All can be managed.

It may seem obvious, but remember that fashionable body shapes come and go. Look at any photo taken at a nightclub in the forties and fifties; many a flabby upper arm* can be seen going to town on the dance floor, no doubt its owner feeling just fine about her appearance.

---

*This is a bit of a non sequitur, but I am reminded of a quote attributed to the last Tsarina of Russia, Empress Alexandra Fyodorovna (1872-1918), referring to the toll nature takes on one's body: "The arms are the last to go." I read this to my mother, who disagreed by responding incredulously, "What was she talking about, a couch?"

Today we gasp because we are constantly told that unless a body part is toned it should be kept, like the crazed first wife of Mr. Rochester, locked away to keep from offending the new governess. This is not a call to reveal all potbellies or don hot pants, but it is a request to keep some perspective when evaluating your flaws.

So:

You are long-waisted with short legs:

The desire is to reduce the impact of the waist and create longer-looking legs. Therefore, high-waisted garments will serve you well. From the waist down, think monochromatic: Pants, belt, and shoes (heels preferably) will benefit by matching, because the effect will be that they are all of one piece. Avoid pants with excessive fullness or cuffs.

You are short-waisted with long legs:

Having long legs is what we call a high-class problem. In other words, it isn't a bad problem to have. The challenge is to visually lower the waistline, thereby mitigating the longer leg and improving overall proportion. If your legs are up to it, by all means show them off. The key is to select tops that skim the torso and hit at the hip. This body type is well served by lower-rise pants and skirts. Just keep those tops on the longish side. Avoid anything that is high-waisted, wide belts (sorry, we love them, too), and any pattern that appears to be horizontal—stripes, obviously, but prints can have a horizontal impact, too.

You are big-busted:

Unless you're Dolly Parton (and if you are, hi, Dolly!), you will desire to reduce the impact of your bust. This is best achieved by trying to visually lengthen the adjacent body parts: the torso and neck. Wear basic, unadorned tops with an open neck or a long, narrow collar and lapel, and, preferably, in dark colors. Wear light-color pants and skirts. Avoid tops that are blouson or voluminous in any way. And please avoid large patterns on top. Remember, you're adorned enough, so keep that top basic! Reducing the impact of the bust does not mean squashing yourself shapeless. Nor does it mean hiding under a perpetual mock turtleneck.

You have a small bust:

There are some individuals who desire to accentuate this feature (like a sophisticated, elegant redhead we know who does it to the hilt!), but most people want to mitigate it. If you are small all over, the issue is not much of a concern; it is only when the bust is small in proportion to the rest of the figure that a problem arises. Here, a wide collar and lapel will serve you well, as will any article of clothing that has breast pockets. You can also sing the blessings of the empire waist (thank you, Empress Josephine), because it was created with you in mind. Halter tops and dresses are also a blessing. Don't shy away from sewing—or having your tailor or dry cleaner sew—an insert into a top with built-in cups. It gives the top a bit more structure and you a bit more fullness.

You have a bit of a tummy . . . or more:

Okay, this is more of a challenge, but there are a number of mitigating options. (We know we use "mitigating" a lot, but it's a good word to use for these circumstances, because these suggestions don't cure, they alleviate.) The objective is to downplay your mid-body by drawing attention to your face and/or your legs. Longer tops like cardigans and tunics are good options, as are longer jackets. Jackets and tops that also have a slight cinch at the waist will enhance the slimming effect, especially from a full-frontal or back view. Regarding dresses, this is another case of the always-forgiving empire waist to the rescue. Skirts and pants should be flat front: no pleats, please! Avoid anything double-breasted or belted or with a waistband. And banish anything even remotely cropped—top, pant, jacket—from your wardrobe!

You have a big butt . . . or more:

Now for the hippier among us. First, think dark colors. That's easy. Skirts can be a friend to your figure, but think flat-front, slightly tapered, and to the knee (exactly where on the knee should be determined by the overall proportions of the skirt to your leg). Pants should be straight-leg and flat front, of course. Tops should emphasize your shoulders and de-emphasize your hips and rear end, so look for a length that falls to the hip, but not at the widest part of your hip—*quel catastrophe!* Avoid anything "extra" that will call attention to this area: no pleats, no ruffles or gathers, no pockets, nothing horizontal, and no large-scale prints. Also, avoid anything heavily textured or novelty in a fabric.

You are height-challenged:

Some of the most stunning women we know are petite. Your figure is perhaps the most challenging to visually lengthen, but it can, indeed, be achieved. High-waisted pants, skirts, and dresses are your friends, as is a monochromatic palette. Look for aspects of clothing construction that give you verticality: center-front seams and princess seams. Avoid tops or jackets that cut you off at the waist, anything pleated, and anything that speaks to a flourish—bows, ruffles, etc. You should also avoid anything cropped.

You are tall:

This is another high-class problem, as long as you embrace it. The greatest challenge for the tall woman is finding things in appropriate lengths. When it comes to pants, it pays to buy the best you can afford. Often the more expensive a pant, the longer it will be. One lesser-known problem area is the wrist—many sleeves are just too short. Do not assume that no one will notice, because someone will. Being tall is great as long as you don't look like a giantess who has outgrown her clothes. Furthermore, stay away from things that are too long and voluminous. Remember Bea Arthur in *Maude?* Fabulous for a forty-seven-year-old female sitcom character in Tuckahoe, New York, but not for you—even if you are a forty-seven-year-old from Tuckahoe.

The Blind Spot: Pay special attention to the fit of outerwear. Most people believe that extra-roominess in coats and jackets is an asset. It's not. It has the potential to make you look like a circus tent. Too many people buy outerwear calculating what size will accommodate their bulkiest article of clothing. If you live at the North Pole, this approach may be appropriate. But under most circumstances, you run the risk of looking like the Incredible Shrinking Woman or the Michelin Tire Man.

Chapter Three

Diagnosing the
Common Closet

The Lesson: What is a closet, really, but a catalogue of the different personas we have auditioned and discarded? Hanging there in our closets are reminders, both good and bad, of who we are, who we've been, and who we've hoped to be. No wonder things can get a bit muddled. In this chapter we will take a two-pronged approach, both practical and theoretical, to getting those racks in order. Think of this chapter as your closet's quest for its authentic self.

"I love America, and I love American women. But there is one thing that deeply shocks me—American closets. I cannot believe one can dress well when you have so much."
—Andrée Putman

Closets are often where we hide things: skeletons, forbidden loves, terrible birthday gifts we couldn't return. It is for this reason that deciding what to wear while staring into those murky depths can be not just daunting, but emotionally exhausting as well. That lace bed-jacket bought at the antique store in Vermont? Those velvet jeans that were already too small the day you picked them out? That cocktail dress purchased especially for the party that was an absolute dud? You remember them all. How could you forget? They stare back at you every time you open your closet door. The time has come to wipe the slate clean and cleanse your sartorial palate.

THE PRACTICAL

Let's begin with the nuts-and-bolts approach to setting your closet on the path to wholeness and health. Presumably, you have read one of the thousands of articles on closet care that seem to spring, fungus-like, from the pages of our popular magazines. Thanks to our culture's current mania for organization and those ubiquitous California Closet★ ads, it seems that the closet should be the centerpiece of one's home. Unless your closet is large enough to receive guests in—and if it is, please think twice about making this a habit—don't fret over a lack of wenge wood shelving and Brunschwig & Fils upholstered poufs. A utilitarian closet is a beautiful thing and absolutely nothing to be ashamed of. What is important is that the closet provides you a relaxed environment from which to select your clothes.

Before we begin the closet-cleansing process, please set aside space for four separate piles. We shall return to these piles, and what goes in them, shortly.

THE THEORETICAL: KIERKEGAARD IN YOUR CLOSET

Who has not suffered that particular depression brought on by a closet full of clothes when one feels that she has nothing to wear? It is our theory that this feeling arises from the discrepancy between your perception of the image your clothing projects and the idealized image

---

★ I'll admit that as a resident of the great city of New York, I have a point of view about closets that has been formed by living here: They are a rare and precious commodity. I've lived in the same apartment for the last fifteen years. It's on the top floor of an 1865 brownstone and contains three closets totaling seven linear feet of hanger space. Consequently, I must employ huge doses of self-discipline in order to stave off Collier Brothers Syndrome, an affliction that turns off the synapses that allow for the editing of clothing and possessions, including newspapers and magazines, and eventually leads to death. Really. And by the way, the Collier brothers lived in NYC. Coincidence? I think not.

you'd like to project in a given situation. The goal is to maximize the correspondence between what you feel conveys the proper image and the items you actually own. This task can only be accomplished when your closet is rid of those items that do not truly make you feel happy and confident when wearing them. This is complex stuff, as you can see. The eternal task of discovering what makes one happy is closely linked to the idea of discovering one's "authentic self." And that's a subject that has preoccupied minds since Cicero worried that laurel wreaths were just so not him.

Søren Kierkegaard (1813–1855), Danish philosopher, opera lover, and the man Ludwig Wittgenstein called "the most profound thinker of the nineteenth century," can actually be a huge help when it comes to curing one's closet. The author of *Fear and Trembling* will not tell you explicitly to toss out those clam diggers, but he will supply two enormously helpful ideas.

We find these two ideas in volume one of Kierkegaard's 1843 book *Either/Or.* The first idea may be clear to you just by reading the preceding sentence. As the title implies, this book is about choice and that is exactly what he suggests you do: Make a choice. In fact, he states that if you do not make choices for yourself, someone else will make them for you. Egad! This simple but powerful idea is not just a life lesson; it is the basis of all personal style. Notice the use of the word "personal." This is not style as dictated—another word for "chosen"—by fashion editors, friends, or pop stars. It is an expression of what speaks to each individual's soul. Listening is not always easy, especially when one's soul demands bell-bottoms in a skinny-jean season. It takes practice and commitment. There may be missteps along the way, but the reward—which is having pride and courage in the convictions of your closet—is worth it.

Ultimately the following process should allow you to divide your closet into four distinct piles.

Choosing what stays and what goes can be intimidating, but we have nothing to fear if we listen to Søren. He counsels that the unmediated choice is the only choice one will never regret. That means no agonizing over whether or not to keep the jumpsuit. If you have to ask, the answer is: Throw it away. If, however, the item causes heart palpitations of happiness, it goes in pile number one:

The Soul-Stirring Pile. Keep in mind that this pile is not just for fantastic items; that flattering cotton tank you love goes in this pile, too.

If a beloved garment needs some attention, put it in **The Repair Pile.** You now have exactly five days to go to the dry cleaner or tailor. Do not allow items to languish. If this is a temptation, perhaps the item is not important enough to fix.

The Give-Away and **The Throw-Out Piles** are where things often get hairy, as in filled with dangers or difficulties. Let's look at what remains in the common closet after the **Soul Stirrers** and **Repairs** have been set aside, and decide what to do about what's left on the rack.

ITEMS THAT DON'T FIT

This is a broad category that ranges from the aforementioned velvet jeans to items that do indeed fit, just not well. There is no reason to have something taking up space in your closet that does not make you feel good. These items must go. Perhaps you like to torture yourself by trying on some jeans from a few years ago to see if you can button them. Clothes do not exist to humiliate their owners. Please do not force garments into performing psychological tasks for which they were not designed. Furthermore, please be kind to yourself. They don't fit. Toss 'em.

ITEMS SO EXPENSIVE YOU FEEL HORRIBLY GUILTY GETTING RID OF THEM

Mistakes were made; find the unloved items a new home. These items are especially pernicious because one remembers the moment of plunking down all that cash or credit every time one glances at them. This can often lead to face-flushing, feelings of unhappiness, and self-recrimination. The goal of this chapter is to remove any closet-based sources of unhappiness, so please, get rid of these items. Since you never wear them, they should be in good condition and therefore avoid the **Throw-Out Pile**. As they hit the **Give-Away Pile,** whisper a solemn oath to not make such silly purchases again. Repeat: Cheap Is Chic, Cheap Is Chic, Cheap Is Chic. There, all better. If you feel you must recoup something and the item retains its value, there are always consignment shops, but eBay is much more *au courant.*

WORK CLOTHES

Perhaps what you wear to work was whisked out of the closet with the items you love. If so, bravo! Many people, especially those who work in more conservative environments, find that a huge chasm stretches between their work and leisure-time looks. Remember Mr. Kierkegaard while surveying your work wardrobe. Do you *choose* to wear the same pair of black slacks as every other woman in your office? Or is it a matter of channeling all your personality into your leisure wardrobe? If you are Agnes Gooch by day and Chita Rivera by night and on the weekends, something must change. There are plenty of ways to bring a little Chita to your nine-to-five. Work can be draining enough without having to wear drab things devoid of any spark. Why not focus on bringing some of those special items you love into your work wardrobe? This is not to say that basics are bad. A beautiful, flattering pair of charcoal gray slacks are a marvel to behold; a deadly dull, ill-fitting suit jacket is not. Notice the use of ill-fitting. If the jacket is deadly dull, fits you well, and makes you feel confident and happy on interviews, that's a whole different deadly dull jacket. We all need practical items, but the key is to make sure they are also great looking and flattering. If you wouldn't want to run into an ex-lover, that's a sure sign you could do better. For the rest of your work wardrobe, if you can't summon more than a "meh," we respectfully suggest you get rid of it.

THOSE ITEMS THAT—FOR REASONS UNKNOWN—YOU NEVER WEAR

Perhaps you try these items on and then hang them back up. Perhaps you skip right over them like something that's been in the freezer so long you no longer want to eat it. You've just said no too many times. Off it goes.

THE ITEM KEPT BECAUSE ONE DAY, IT MAY BE CHIC AGAIN

There is no look so strange or unflattering that it will not be recycled. These days it seems to happen with stunning alacrity. Many a woman scoffed at the idea that leggings would ever return, and here they are, back with a vengeance. However, one only has so much space and one never knows if you'll find a trend equally compelling on the next (or third or fourth) go round. Better to move on.

SCENES OF FORMER TRIUMPHS

These are items that you would never, ever wear but keep for purely sentimental reasons. The T-shirt that reads HAPPY SIXTIETH, IRV! or the ratty sweater you were wearing when you got into graduate school. Yes, they remind you of wonderful times, but they have to go. Irv's birthday will live on in your memory, as will the thrill of receiving that fat envelope. Let the physical items go on to new adventures. You'll retain the wonderful memories *and* more shelf space. It's a win/win situation!

THE REPEATS, REDUXES, AND REPRISES

Perhaps you find nothing as restful as a day spent at your local mall, fighting the crowds for yet another cardigan because … who doesn't need twelve black angora cardigans? If you shop like a drunken sailor, chances are that you own far more than you will ever be able to wear. This leads to Creeping Closet Syndrome—the sad state of affairs in which your wardrobe takes over your home.*

EXCEPTIONS

We are loath to admit it, but in certain very rare cases it is permissible to keep a piece that is never worn. We've all asked older relatives why they didn't hold on to that fabulous outfit we've seen in photos. It is permissible to keep something for posterity. However, it is highly unlikely that more than one piece per closet overhaul is worthy of preservation for the sake of unborn grandchildren. Assess with a keen eye.

If radical shape-shifting is going on—a diet or pregnancy—of course it makes sense to hold on to items that will soon fit again. Be honest, though. If those last ten pounds have been on their way out for the last ten years, why not make room in the closet for things that will fit now? Carpe diem!

Are you ready? Begin! Toss, toss, toss into the **Give-Away Pile**. It is surprising how liberating divesting oneself of old outfits can be. You are allowing your closet

---

* I've witnessed this firsthand. My mother built a beautiful house on the Delaware shore (the Hamptons of the Mid-Atlantic) and it is chockablock with closets. She lives alone, and is nothing if not neat, yet there is no room in either closets or dressers for me to put anything when I visit.
  Here is the context: She built a two-story house that allows for her to live on the first floor exclusively. The second floor consists of a loft overlooking the living room and foyer. There are two closets in the loft, plus a doorway to a large attic space. There are two guest bedrooms, each of which has a large closet. Every closet is *full*. A couple of years ago, I purged the attic of unnecessary things, so my mother was left with an orderly and open space. When I returned the following Christmas, she asked me to put away her decorations before I left. When I opened the door to the attic, I let out a cry of anguish. She had installed a closet rod that ran the length of the room—and that rod was full of clothes on hangers. AHHHHHHH!!!

to represent who you are *now*. You've just gotten better and better, why not let your closet come along, too?

WHAT YOU LOVE

Well done! The wheat and chaff have been parted. Only delightful pieces should remain. Now that they are all mingling together and not lost in the closet, look for a connection, a narrative through-line. In other words, is there something that the pieces you love have in common? Bright colors, marabou trim? Sumptuous fabrics and shades of gray? Sometimes seeing all of one's favorites grouped together can be a bit of a shock. One may think of herself as a Jackie Bouvier type, but her most beloved pieces are more like burlesque star Tempest Storm. What to do?

First, congratulations—your soul has spoken! A discovery has been made. Look closely at the pieces. What do they have in common? Is it a shared silhouette? Are they waist enhancing or perhaps light and ethereal? What the pieces have in common can be thought of as their form. If, for instance, favored pieces tend toward the ethereal, it does not mean that dressing head-to-toe like a fairy is a good idea. It means that incorporating pieces light of form will ensure that you are happy when the closet door opens. Let us now return to Mr. Kierkegaard for the second of his two important ideas.

Imagine a gin martini served in a pint glass or a Wagnerian opera–version of *Sex and the City*. Both might have their . . . *intoxicating* charms, but neither would be a flawless fit. The martini would be undrinkable because it would get warm much faster than you could quaff it. The glass the martini is served in is an essential part of the martini itself. Carrie Bradshaw wouldn't be nearly as much fun if she and Mr. Big both drank a magic potion and sang the same infernal love duet for four hours. The thirty-minute television format is the ideal medium for her banter and romance.

So should it be for you and your clothes. For Kierkegaard, a "classic" results when form and content meet in perfect harmony. In our case, the content is the person inside the garment; the form is the garment itself. Some form and content marriages are quite obvious. Examples that come to mind are Paris Hilton and the line Heatherette, or Audrey Hepburn and Givenchy. Rarely, if ever, have those four names appeared in the same sentence. Nonetheless, what is important is that the particular strengths of the content—Paris and Audrey —are showcased by the form. What isn't successful is choosing a rigid form and trying to wedge one's unhappy content into it. If one is lucky enough to have a Monica Bellucci-esque figure, wearing a Hedi Slimane Dior man's suit might be difficult. Borrowing androgynous elements while respecting the line of one's figure, though, will be chic. A more quotidian example might be the financial consultant who goes to work every day in black slacks and pumps, but loves anything related to ballet. By switching those black slacks for a softer, slightly full skirt, paired with a slim black turtleneck and a belt at her true waist, she can bring some of the form she loves into play without sacrificing loyalty to her content.

"Yes, yes," you say, "form and content are fine, but what about this collection of soul-stirring clothes now outside of my closet?" Lovely question! Those are your clothes for the next seven days. Each day you must wear one soul-stirring item. Think of it as strength training for the style muscles. Too often we "save" things we love for a special occasion; as a result we rarely wear the very things we love best. Perhaps that silk slip dress could go to work with black tights, flats, and a cashmere cardigan. Throw that sparkly cardigan on over a tank top and jeans. Just get them in the rotation. The confidence you'll gain is the reward for all your hard work.

The Blind Spot: If getting rid of things were easy, there wouldn't be an overstuffed closet to be found. After you have assembled your Soul-Stirring Pile, take another look. Does everything deserve to be there? Be ruthless. If the thought of giving away an item that was so fun five years ago makes you sad, by all means grieve. Then get rid of it.

Chapter Four

The Fashion Mentor:
Beyond Audrey

The Lesson: It seems there is a dearth of fashion icons available. We are always surprised that magazines trot out the same people year after year: Rich hippie? Paging Talitha Getty! Mediterranean siren? Forty-year-old photo of Sophia Loren, coming up! American aristocrat? Jaqueline Kennedy Onassis, *bien sur!* Fashion editors often include a list of pieces that will "help you get the look." Truly, could anything be sillier? These women were very much products of their time and place and "getting their look" really means putting on a costume. Are Talitha, Sophia, and Jackie worth studying? Yes. However, what is far more helpful than asking you to gaze upon the same pictures of the same—albeit fabulous—women is coming up with some new inspirations! This is not to discount the idea that you can—and should—learn about style from others. The problem is that the selection of role models has become, well, a little tired. By providing a new selection—some whom you will know well, some whom you may not—we hope to find you a style mentor who actually works for who you are.

"Why not be one's self?
That is the whole secret of a successful appearance.
If one is a greyhound, why try to look like a Pekinese?"
—Edith Sitwell

THE DIFFERENCE BETWEEN AN ICON AND A MENTOR

In order to become a fashion icon, one has to be seen. Simple enough, but it means that the people who become icons are in professions—or marriages—that dictate a lot of time in front of the camera. Since a certain type of personality is drawn to professions that result in photos in *Us Weekly* or *Vogue,* it can be difficult to translate their looks to an existence beyond the red carpet. We are also living at a time when stylists have replaced fairy godmothers as the agents of choice for helping starlets become princesses. Since you are much more than a blank body with a show on FOX, we will be looking at some women who have style and character. Keep the word "character" in mind.

The women who follow are not *icons* like Jackie or Audrey, but they can certainly be fashion *mentors.*

The best way to utilize a style mentor is to be inspired to investigate and experiment. This list is not prescriptive, as in, you must choose one of these looks and everything will be fine. Nor is it an exercise in historical reenactment or a foray into anthropology. You may work in an environment where djellabas are not appropriate, but that doesn't mean you can't have a bit of Tangiers in your cubicle. Or, if your lifestyle *is* more djellaba-friendly,

but you prefer the ultra-glam Washington, D.C., look of Deeda Blair, you can keep the sharpness—and incredible hair—without buying couture. Before you book that twice-weekly roller set at the salon, keep one thing in mind: There is, in American culture, a premium placed on being "nice." Although this can make life easier in many ways, it is simply hell for developing style. Style requires a "like it or lump it" attitude toward one's public. Your public includes husbands, wives, girlfriends, boyfriends, mothers, children, workmates, classmates, and the people who pass you on the street. You do not exist to win their approval. Does this mean we think you should wear a cocktail dress and saddle shoes to work because that's what you love? Well, let us invoke the Blackstone Ratio: "Better that ten guilty persons escape than that one innocent suffers." In other words, if adjusting to and discovering your personal style results in a few funny outfits, so be it. What is important is that a space is created for a person to embrace who she truly is. Even if, and it pains us to write this, it includes saddle shoes.

THE MENTORS

As we put this list together, it became obvious that one thing tied these women together: They always look like themselves. And what an achievement that is, to remain unswayed by the hurricanes of trend and the maelstroms of media hype. Although we've placed each of our mentors in a certain category, many cross back and forth.

LES FRANÇAISES

Carine Roitfeld—Charlotte Gainsbourg—Catherine Deneuve
The French are "like it or lump it" practitioners *par excellence.* They do not share the American lust for sweetness and light, and as a result, their stylish women often have an edge that their counterparts here lack. This is not so much about the particular pieces they wear, but the way they are worn and the way they fit. Take for example Carine Roitfeld, Editor-in-Chief of French *Vogue.* This former model and stylist rims her eyes in black, has striking brows, and has entirely unfussy shoulder-length hair. Looking through photos, you cannot miss the fact that whether she is in a huge fur jacket or a button-down, she radiates sex and a certain toughness. She is also over fifty. Unlike so many of her contemporaries in the fashion world, she does not look like a big evening out for her might include some dry toast and demitasse of Evian. Ms. Roitfeld looks ready to have a smoke, a vodka, and a roll in the hay. Bravo!

Charlotte Gainsbourg is the child of two stars—the late, great Serge Gainsbourg and the English singer and actress Jane Birkin. It was for Jane that the Hermès "Birkin bag" was created, supposedly to hold Charlotte's diapers. How could she *not* grow up to be stylish? Now in her early thirties, Charlotte does that French hair thing like nobody else. French hair, for some reason, looks best dirty and undone. With the hair, her obvious intelligence, and a wardrobe of classic pieces—trench coat, black dress, menswear-inspired looks—she manages to achieve what eludes so many: effortless chic. In a sense, she bridges the gap between Ms. Roitfeld and the following mentor, Catherine Deneuve.

Ahhh, the bridges of Paris! Catherine Deneuve is simply a gorgeous person. But for us, what is important is how she styles herself. Classic, classic, classic. Straight out of the 7th you might say—the arrondissement of quiet money and privilege—her wardrobe, then and now, sets off her beauty rather than fights it. Think of her as Séverine in *Belle de Jour*. First, you see Ms. Deneuve, then those fabulous Yves Saint Laurent clothes. Spare and graphic, her garments aren't crying out for attention like a needy toddler. Ms. Deneuve is free to project an unbridled sexiness, while always being absolutely regal. She is an ice princess, but one who could burn you.

Signature Look

This look, like so many, is actually a state of mind. It is entirely correct—the dress fits beautifully—but it does not vie for approbation. This can feel strange to the woman who feels casually dressed unless she is in something revealing. In other words, there are more ways to seduce than by removing most of your clothes before heading out for the evening. French women dress to send the message they intend to send. So, sleep a few nights on that hair, throw on a knee-length black skirt and a trench coat, spritz your neck with a little Eau du Soir, and have a glass of wine at lunch. *Merde,* why not allow *les petites* to have a sip as well? How else will they develop their palates?

THE SIRENS

Angelina Jolie—Nigella Lawson—Julie Christie

These are the women who make you want to lock up your menfolk. They are sexy, yes, but there is something else that vaults them into the realm of irresistibility. By the way, if you haven't read it, plan to pick up *The Odyssey* for your next beach vacation. What an adventure! It has monsters, suitors, shepherds—and most important—sirens. The sirens were half-avian maidens who lured sailors with their enchanting songs, causing the poor mariners to wreck their ships. Although causing a maritime disaster might be a bit much, who doesn't like the idea of being fatally irresistible? One might assume that sirens are born and not made, but the ways of the siren can be cultivated. What becomes a siren most is a combination of carnality and . . . something else. Take for instance Angelina Jolie. Yes, she is extremely impressive physically, but what elevates her to siren status is her air of machisma. She flies a plane and sports a Cartier Tank watch like nobody's business. She rarely deviates from her classic, menswear-inspired pieces. In that respect, her wardrobe makes her eligible for honorary Française status—the great trousers, the simple black tees and sweaters that allow her to always look great, even in those paparazzi shots. She's a sexy, sophisticated woman rather than a cream puff. Perhaps you like the cream puff idea, though, without the tattoos and leather pants. In that case, we offer Nigella Lawson.

Nigella Lawson is the lushly figured British television chef. Although she has that aforementioned figure, a throaty voice, and a lovely face, she writes—and cooks—with wit and intelligence. That's what elevates her to siren status. And all those smiles and moans of pleasure while cooking don't hurt, either. One quality that all sirens share is that they are capable of taking a sensual pleasure in the things around them. This is why the siren often gravitates to cashmere, leather, and silk garments. It does not mean, though, that the siren must spend her day in a peignoir. Ms. Lawson opts for simple, fitted tops and dark bottoms. Her sweaters are tight, yes, but the judicious deployment of foundation garments keeps everything smooth and bump-free.

Another siren to investigate is the actress Julie Christie. Surely you've seen *Doctor Zhivago*. If not, please do, even though according to acclaimed critic Edward Said's memoir, Omar Sharif was not a very nice schoolboy. What is important for our purposes is the absolutely radiant Lara, played by Ms. Christie. This is a siren with incredible dignity and a fabulous fur hat. Any style fan should acquaint herself, really, with all of Ms. Christie's work from the '60s and '70s. Not only is *Darling* chockablock with wonderful sixties looks, it's a valuable cautionary tale for anyone, male or female, who is considering becoming a trophy wife.

Signature Look

It's all in the eyes. Often sirens have a look in their eyes that says they are fascinated by something, and few things are as attractive as passionate interest. Whether it is food or the impending arrival of the Bolsheviks, the siren has something on her mind, something beyond what she is wearing. While awakening the siren within, you must cultivate an air of devil-may-care. Try a body-conscious wrap dress, but invest in a supportive bra and control-top hosiery. The key is to understand that you are in control of your body *and* how much of it you choose to reveal.

MASCULIN/FEMININ

Katharine Hepburn—Coco Chanel

These are the women who make you want to lock up your menfolk *and* your womenfolk. This is a look that blurs the gender distinction. Instead of menswear-inspired looks, this category of dressers may just opt for actual menswear. That is not to say that the goal is to look just like a man, quite the opposite. This category plays with the provocative contrast between the signals sent by masculine clothes and the female body that is wearing them. Furthermore, it takes a powerful, confident woman to pull off a cummerbund. And we all know that confidence and power make up a particularly potent cocktail of erotic attractiveness. The fact that our culture's

current vocabulary of femininity is rather limited makes this look all the more radical. So radical, in fact, that we must turn to the past to come up with the most famous examples.

Standing loafers and wingtips above the competition is Katharine Hepburn. She scandalized Hollywood with her trousers, but forever won a place in the fashion pantheon. Her brisk Yankee beauty was unmistakable in golf clothes or evening gowns. Talk about owning a look! Who else could make a whole *style* of top—the turtleneck—so unmistakably theirs?

Many of the items we consider unisex today were once squarely in the menswear category. We can thank Coco Chanel for fixing that situation. Part of her masculine mystique had to do with using untraditional fabrics—fabrics associated exclusively with menswear, like wool flannel and wool jersey (the latter being associated with mens' undergarments). She was also a stylist extraordinaire: She raided the closets of her lovers and restyled their jackets and shirts to suit herself. Physically, she set herself apart as well, with chicly cropped hair and a tan when the very idea of getting sun was strictly verboten for the upper classes. But Chanel's *big* menswear nod (and the sole article of apparel that branded her as being masculine) were her trousers—yet another scandal! What is it that people find so frightening about a woman wearing the pants? That's a whole other book, but what is important is that this look retains its charge today.

Signature Look

This is an easy one. First, find a crisp oxford-cloth shirt with light starch. It will work with everything and play nicely with overtly feminine pieces, like full skirts. Second, visit the other perfume counter. Gender differences in perfume are nothing more than a marketing choice. Dabble a bit. You'll be pleased.

LES GAMINES

Sofia Coppola—Natalie Portman

Classic, feminine, and young. Sounds a bit like a law firm, doesn't it? In this case, though, it is the writer and director Sofia Coppola we are discussing. Petite with extremely striking features, Ms. Coppola actually managed to look cool winning an Oscar. Yes, there may be some factors that make it tempting to dismiss her—the extremely famous family, her close relationship with Marc Jacobs— but let's be fair, who couldn't use a little bit of her sartorial sangfroid? In a recent article in *The New York Times Magazine,* she led a walk around Paris in simple black ballet flats, a black pleated skirt, and a navy pullover. In another photo she appeared in jeans and a black crewneck sweater. One does not get the sense that she agonized that morning over what to wear. That is not to say she looked sloppy or underdone. She looks great and comfortable in her clothing and her skin. She is an excellent example of a modern gamine.

Another contemporary gamine is the absolutely lovely Natalie Portman. Ms. Portman, too, is petite, which raises the issue of whether petite-ness is a prerequisite for being gaminesque. Well, from a strictly etymological standpoint, the answer would be yes, since the French word as a noun refers to a child or adolescent. However, it also means "mischievous" or "impish." We believe you can be mischievous and impish at any size. Ms. Portman manages to look both sophisticated and age-appropriate despite her petite stature. She favors simple shapes in a muted color palette. Her choices almost always fall within the realm of classic, while never being stuffy.

Signature Look

Ahh, those French, here they are again. The key to this look is simplicity. For warm weather: a basic shift and ballet flats or leather sandals. And for the winter: pretty much the same but with seasonally appropriate fabrics.

Flat boots, wool tights, ballet slippers. The gamine is rarely seen in a heel.

THE RISK TAKERS

Kate Moss—Sarah Jessica Parker—Chloe Sevigny

This category is subtitled "You Laugh Now, But You'll Buy Later." These are the ladies who dwell in the cold and lonely peaks of fashion. Yes, the air is purer up there, but sometimes the folks at sea level just don't get these looks. Give it a year, though, and everyone at zero elevation will be clamoring for leggings. Sometimes the elevation leads to choices by these ladies that are just, shall we say, *too* challenging, and all the lowland dwellers and their blogs go crazy over what they wore to that gala. This is the risky part of being a risk taker. But she plows ahead knowing that in many cases, time, and the buyers at Barneys, will vindicate her.

Kate Moss in gray skinny jeans tucked into slouchy boots, and a fitted waistcoat. Sarah Jessica Parker in formal shorts and stilettos. Chloe Sevigny in high-waisted pants and a vintage satin blouse. Need we say more?

Signature Look

We can admire, but we cannot endorse. The risk taker approach is simply too risky for a layperson. That said, one big or striking fashion item, if worn in isolation, is permissible. Take for instance the white furry boots Kate Moss was seen wearing on Fifth Avenue . . . nine years ago, just in from Reykjavik. So if on your next trip to Iceland you fall passionately in love with a hat adorned with antlers—bring it home. But dipping the toes into the crystalline waters of risk must be a slow process. Which means, if you're wearing the antler hat, you must leave the caribou vest at home.

THE ROCKERS

Patti Smith—Cat Power

Stripped-down and soulful, Patti Smith has not changed her clothes since 1973. Surely the garments themselves have changed, but her look has remained the same. If rock and roll is, or once was, about pushing the envelope, Ms. Smith could be said to have gnawed the envelope before spitting it on the first three rows. Although her baggy jeans, T-shirt or button-down *sans* bra, and men's blazer is not a look for everyone—or anyone, really, save her—

she is an excellent sartorial inspiration. Three decades ago, la Smith found a look that worked beautifully for her and has stayed faithful. We should all be so wise. Viva la Smith!

And now for a rocker born three decades ago: the singer-songwriter Chan Marshall, who performs as Cat Power. Continuing the rock tradition of loving denim, Ms. Marshall is most often in jeans and either a tank or a plaid shirt. "How thrilling," you mutter. But look again: She chooses pieces that subtly show her figure and she offsets her utilitarian clothing choices with heavy bangs and eyeliner. It makes the whole thing more Françoise Hardy than farmhand. Ms. Marshall is a great example of a boyish, even gamine look on a woman who is neither boyish nor tiny.

Signature Look

These women wear denim that is sexy because it still retains a little of its blue-collar past. This means you actually have a chance to break in a pair of raw denim jeans. This is also a look about loyalty. Your favorite T-shirt becomes your only T-shirt. Take something extremely basic and make it your own, just as these women have taken unconventional looks and lives and made them art.

THE BOHEMIANS

Beatrice Wood— Edith Bouvier Beale—Donna Karan

This is the category for the woman who loves to layer. Whether it is strand after strand of beads, wrists a-jingle with bangles, or a snappy sweatshirt head-wrap, for the bohemian, more is always more.

Beatrice Wood, who died in 1998 at age 105, was a potter who lived in Ojai, an orange blossom–scented bastion of bohemia in the mountains of Southern California. A protégé and lover of Marcel Duchamp, Ms. Wood is renowned for her work as well as her liberated lifestyle. Just as she adorned her pots with layers of beautiful lustre glaze, Ms. Wood adorned herself in layers of luminous textiles, topped off by hands and wrists decorated with jewelry, and bright red lips. Her philosophy of life and work drew from both East and West, and her wardrobe followed suit. Her memoir *I Shock Myself* is a wonderful read.

Edith Bouvier Beale had none of Ms. Wood's artistic accomplishment or freedom, but she just might be more famous. If you haven't seen the Maysles Brothers' documentary *Grey Gardens,* you absolutely must. Bump *Doctor Zhivago* if you have to. The film is not only riveting, it is a fashion touchstone, season after season. Edie was Jackie Bouvier Kennedy's first cousin. She lived with her mother at a compound, Grey Gardens, in East Hampton, New York. Surrounded by cats and raccoons, the two women play out a mother-daughter power struggle that has been going on for fifty years. Through it all, Little Edie, as she is called, is clad in the most spectacularly odd outfits that she creates herself. Her famous "Revolutionary Costume" involves a pair of girdle shorts over nude hose with a skirt fashioned out of a piece of brown material that, as she helpfully offers, can be worn as a cape as well. This is a simple transition because the "skirt" is fastened on with safety pins. On top she wears a brown fitted turtleneck and a black sweater as a head-wrap pinned under her chin. This is certainly eccentric, but many a designer has cribbed from Ms. Beale. The film is also an excellent cautionary tale for those who feel there is no harm in moving home. Suddenly, thirty years have passed and you are wearing flea collars around your ankles.

In a raccoon-free home also in East Hampton dwells another bohemian, the mega-designer Donna Karan. Although her work has provided a wardrobe for a whole generation of chic working women, Ms. Karan is now an excellent mentor for the polished bohemian looking for something a bit less far out. Present in her wardrobe are all the bohemian favorites—flowing skirts, layered jewelry—but done with enough restraint that she looks like she just came from the beach, not a gypsy caravan.

Signature Look

The bohemian draws from many sources; there is often an ethnic component to the look. A bohemian standby to avoid is the fringed silk shawl that only pianos should wear. While ethnic is great, folkloric is to be avoided. The idea is eclectic, not travelogue.

This world is wide, so feel free to venture into it with as little as an arm full of bangles—or both arms full of bangles . . . and your antler hat.

LES DOYENNES

Deeda Blair —Pauline de Rothchild—Lee Radziwell
Doyennes are not born doyennes. They ascend to this status of quality, taste, and style. Doyennes are haughty, monied, attenuated, and of the highest rank. When speaking about such nobility, one has to reach beyond the

clothes, because it is the context embracing the doyenne that offers the full picture.

Owing to the Washington, D.C., roots of one of us, we must pay homage to a Mrs. William McCormack Blair Jr. Though she was an undisputed society leader who presided over one of the grandest salons in the nation's capital, she was also Vice President of the Lasker Foundation. This was no mere lady who lunches.*

What was particularly fascinating about Mrs. Blair was her hair. It was the biggest 'do ever, complete with Cruella De Vil coloring, but it was stunning, not ridiculous. In her heydey, she was the *ne plus ultra* of D.C. glamour and sophistication, even during the 1,000 glamour-embossed Kennedy days. Forgive us for speaking about Mrs. Blair in the past tense. We know that she remains active and visible: We just saw her in a society column that described her arrival at a benefit being accompanied by a European royal. In the corresponding photograph, she appears infinitely more regal than her titled escort. It's not just her beautiful clothes and impeccable grooming; it's her carriage. Mrs. Blair's posture is Vreeland-like—ramrod straight. But she's never stiff. She glides across a room as if powered by a small engine under her feet.

Grace Mirabella, who reigned for seventeen years at *Vogue* and later launched *Mirabella,* has said Mrs. Blair would seek her counsel about the couture collections: "What do you think about this dress, Grace?" Yes, Mrs.

---

* Her large Georgetown house was decorated with an elegance and taste that was new to me as a child: coromandel screens, buttery painted walls, heavy gilt mirrors, and beige suede upholstery. Hers was a D.C. version of Chanel's apartment on the Rue Cambon.

Blair was one of the few reliable supporters of couture, but for every $30,000 dress she bought, she would donate ten times that amount to a charitable organization. From the House of Dior to the Memorial Sloan-Kettering Cancer Center, people genuflect to her. That's a remarkable achievement.

Pauline de Rothchild was born Pauline Potter in the doyenne-hatching town of Baltimore (also the birthplace of the Duchess of Windsor, and Nancy Lancaster of Colefax and Fowler fame), Ms. Potter headed north to New York and landed a position at Hattie Carnegie. Her superb breeding and finishing-school education prepared her well for the social circles into which she would ascend.

When she worked professionally, Ms. Potter was always clad in a suit: a high-waisted pencil skirt with a shrunken jacket, thereby accentuating her height (she was always the tallest woman in the room), her slim figure, and her aristocratic carriage. After becoming the Baroness de Rothchild, her clothing became quite flamboyant (something fierce was hiding under that demure suit). And she was never a fashion victim; that is, she was a self-stylist who mixed unlikely prints and wore mink-lined trench coats (a first) with ballet flats to the opera.

Lee Radziwill, "The Princess" before her divorce, was the more tightly wound of the Bouvier sisters. She is the only one of our doyennes whom we suspect would creak with every movement of her meticulously sculpted jacket or dress. If we attribute "girly" to Pauline de Rothchild, then "deftly tailored" is appropriate for Lee Radziwill. With the exception of a lace veil, she's seldom seen in anything other than suits, A-line sheaths, and capri pants. Neither her grooming nor her clothes are ever anything other than perfect. While these characteristics can be intimidating, they account for her sublime grandness. There is an aura about her that goes beyond her bloodline and her celebrity. She exudes an elegance and a confidence that is overpowering.

Signature Look

To be blunt, the doyenne is about power. Hers is a look that underscores the doyenne's place in the world and, accordingly and not surprisingly, this can cause others to writhe—and shrink—in their seats. Suits suit the doyenne, but not any ol' suit. The Yves Saint Laurent power suit of the '70s is the classical centerpiece of the doyenne's wardrobe.

If you aspire to this look, keep your friends close and your enemies closer! This is the hyper-polished, utterly correct, dress-to-the-nines look that must be executed from sun-up till bedtime. It requires an extraordinary commitment—not a once a week flirtation—otherwise you run the risk of people thinking you're a drag queen!

ITALIAN AND COMPLICATED
The Women of Antonioni and Fellini

Here's where you can get your Sophia Loren fix, along with the likes of Claudia Cardinale and Monica Vitti. For Antonioni and Fellini, women are often dominant and full of style and sexuality. And teased hair. Even in the murk-filled world of Antonioni's *Il Grido,* the women smolder.

As one of them lives in a hut, that's really saying something. Think of them trudging through the marshy lowlands of the Po River Valley, glaring at the empty beach in Rimini, or silently sailing around the cold waters of Sicily. You, too, can achieve their sexy brand of despair. Don't let the fact that you wear a size 14 and are from Guyana dictate your ability to wear this Mediterranean look. Anyone can don a curvaceous black skirt and a belted wool cardigan.

Signature Look

The key look here is all about hair and eyelashes. Both of them should be prodigious. An ample bosom is suggested, but not required. Think about a thin camisole or slip underneath a fitted skirt or housedress. This is womanhood straining to break free from her bonds—or her peasant top.

POWER BROKERS

Martha Stewart—Vanessa Redgrave—Oprah Winfrey

We would be remiss if we were not to address a high-powered executive of style, and who better than Martha Stewart. One of this book's key messages is, "own your look," and, indeed, Martha does. A former fashion model turned style guru *par excellence*, Martha Stewart epitomizes casual elegance. Whether she's gathering eggs in the chicken coop, planting an herb garden, or baking a soufflé, she's appropriately garbed. Tweeds, flannels, and cottons are her mainstay. And other than black-tie benefits (or court appearances), she prefers a pant paired with a blouson top. Some attribute Martha's clear view of her style self as emanating from her modeling days, but we maintain that the elements of quality, taste, and style that govern her lifestyle determine her fashion. After all, what is fashion without lifestyle and vice versa?

Vanessa Redgave, from *Blow-Up* on, managed to retain her steely reserve while being a red-hot mama. There is something in the tension between her patrician beauty and carriage and her obvious sensuality. She has managed to maintain this beautifully—she does not shy away from aging, but rather embraces it and dresses accordingly. Her clothes are luxurious and structured—they befit a woman her age while not aging her at all.

Oprah Winfrey is a prime example of someone who always looks polished. Her hair, makeup, and all of her clothing are exquisite—she gleams! The way this look is attained is by wearing well-cut, beautifully designed, gorgeous fabrics.

Signature Look

This is a look that stresses quality over quantity—well-structured, tailored, and in the most sumptuous fabrics you can afford. These are women, not girls throwing an evening's outfit together.

The Blind Spot: It's important to note that there is a difference between homage and parody. While we encourage you to draw inspiration from your favorite mentors, this does not give you free rein to dress as an Angelina Jolie or Martha impersonator. Real style is achieved when accenting your signature look with one of theirs.

Chapter Five

Shoulders Back: Style from the Inside Out

The Lesson: No matter how spectacular a look, if the person inside it is bent, lopsided, crumpled, or otherwise hunched, there is simply no saving it. Far too many people, men and women alike, are walking around completely unaware that with a few simple adjustments they could look and feel immeasurably better. It's time to straighten up and fly right.

*"It is only shallow people who do not judge by appearances.
The true mystery of the world is the visible, not the invisible."*
—Oscar Wilde

One complaint that many, many women have is that fashion is designed only to be worn by sixteen-year-old Slovenian sylphs. This is, of course, a huge generalization, but it highlights a problem. We are repeatedly asked why designers don't do more for the shorter, rounder, or older among us. The tone of the question often suggests that the asker is being hampered in her quest for style because of the limited clothing choices available to her. There are a plethora of reasons why the fashion business runs the way it does, and change in this area does not seem too imminent. So why not look at it this way: While it is true that the farther one gets from sample size—the standard size designers work with—the more limited the selection of on-trend looks becomes, this is not necessarily a terrible loss. In fact, it forces one to let go of the idea of fashion and truly embrace her personal style. So, a bit of tough love. We cannot control what designers, magazine editors, and advertisers are going to foist on us next. What we can control is the way we present ourselves. In this chapter we will discuss how to get the most important element in any look—the person inside it—simply glowing with chic.

THE SHOULDER FALLACY

Everybody has been ordered to "Put your shoulders back" by a mother, teacher, or drill sergeant. And how do we comply? We push our shoulder blades back and together with all our might. This position is sustainable for the moment it takes to march out of sight of the authority figure. Once we are alone again, we release our shoulders to their habitually rounded position and slink away. What a tragedy! No one wants bad posture, but the idea of maintaining that uncomfortable "shoulders back" position is unrealistic and far from pleasant. For some, the rounded shoulders act as camouflage, a spine-injuring attempt to deflect notice away from a large bust or tall height. Perhaps you are familiar with "Tall Girl Slump." The trouble is, posture telegraphs the slumper's feelings of discomfort and insecurity, making her far more likely to be noticed by those who might wish to take advantage of such a feeling. The well-positioned shoulder tells the world that you are a confident, healthy individual—not a showboat or a dormouse.

Although adopting correct posture habits takes time, the process is not painful and the benefits are immediate. The first, absolutely ironclad rule may seem strange, but here it is: Forget about putting your shoulders back.

Well-positioned shoulders are not achieved by actually putting them "back." Instead, you must do the following: Focus on pulling the shoulders away from the ears. Imagine drawing the shoulder blades down the back and allowing the collarbone to be as open as possible without thrusting the breast forward. At no time should the shoulder blades be pinned together. This position makes keeping the head perfectly balanced on the neck far easier. This means you'll sail through life and into old age with a limber body and not a trace of a dowager's hump. Have you ever heard of a dowager's hump? This outdated but evocative phrase refers to a curvature of the spine that produces a lump of flesh between the shoulder blades. The curvature is a product of osteoporosis and contributes to the impression of shrinking as one ages. No one likes to shrink, so work on those shoulders.

GETTING ALIGNED

Imagine a model skeleton hanging in a very chic laboratory. The skeleton is held together by wires and a pole that travels from its base, through the cavity between the pelvic bones, along the spine, and up into the skull. Try standing in front of a mirror and imagining yourself suspended in the same manner. Yes, a bit macabre, but a helpful exercise nonetheless. Does your pole travel gracefully up into your skull? Or does it poke out of your neck because your head juts forward? Is the pole knocking into the back of your pelvis because you stand with your stomach thrust out? Is the pole too long because you allow your ribs to sag into your diaphragm, shortening your torso? The best way to make sure that your skeleton is giving you its all is by remembering that just as in clothing, the line is what is important. Nothing on our model skeleton is crunched together or sticking out to the side. The skeleton looks relaxed, ready to samba or hit a tennis ball.

The body is engineered to function in the most efficient manner possible. That means that aches and pains can be avoided if the skeleton is given plenty of room to work. It also means a youthful, attractive silhouette really should have very little to do with age. For some reason, many American women insist on foreshortening themselves by allowing their shoulders to round forward, their ribs to sink toward their pelvis, and their heads to hang forward heavily. This difference is rarely mentioned in that endless debate of why French women are chic, but it is worth noting. What often gets chalked up to a certain hauteur in the French is partially the impression given by proper alignment of the body. Dior's new look does not work if one is slumped over and drooling. Nor does one see many photos of Catherine Deneuve standing with her stomach sticking out and her shoulders rounded. So the question is: How does one go about getting things to line up? By starting with the pelvis.

One of the most helpful pieces of advice on the subject comes from a wonderful book called *Your Carriage, Madam* by Janet Lane. Though published in 1934, it is not in the least bit dated, perhaps because the temptation to slump is eternal. Ms. Lane suggests that in order to bring the pelvis into proper alignment, one should imagine slipping between two tables at a crowded restaurant. Instinctively, one tucks one's bottom under and draws the navel into the spine. This is the proper position for one's pelvis. Since French bistros are usually packed and their tables are only inches apart, one can think of proper pelvic alignment as the "bistro position." If one is familiar with pilates, it is also immediately recognizable as the "scooped" position that is the backbone of that fitness method. This ever-so-slight pelvic tilt keeps the bottom from jutting out and flattens the stomach. Not only does it make one look slimmer and taller, it provides support for the lower back. The change it makes to one's seated posture is also tremendous. Next time you are seated at a desk, try slipping into bistro posture. It naturally brings the spine into contact with the chair and makes it far easier to pull those shoulders down. All of this means less fatigue, which means more time for productive work. Or more efficient work—which means potentially leaving the office early! The benefits of good posture are manifold!

OUT AND ABOUT

One of the joys of living in New York, as both authors of this book do, is that you can walk anywhere. The sidewalks are perpetually filled with people hurrying about. The rich, the poor, the glamorous, and the frumpy all jostle for space on the same few feet of sidewalk. Observing this pageant of humanity, it becomes clear that despite all of our differences, the vast majority of people have one thing in common: They are terrible walkers. One can see it all—clumpers and shufflers, weavers and waddlers. It's not just on city sidewalks, either. We cannot forget a day spent on a gorgeous beach this past summer watching a parade of swimsuit-clad bodies traipse by. The problems weren't the bikinied and betrunked physiques; it was the way their owners dragged themselves up and down the sand. You'd think they were on their way to the gallows, not lunch and a glass of rosé. These were people who had obviously invested time at the gym, and plenty of money at Eres. Yet the whole effect they'd worked to achieve was undone by the simple act of walking. Far, far better to be softer of tone but walking with one's head and neck in proper alignment than to be a hunched person with visible stomach muscles.

So much of the information we take in about another person is transmitted subconsciously, and few things say more about us than the way we get ourselves from place to place. The person who moves gracefully is immediately more attractive, regardless of their physical characteristics. Grace, and the idea of cultivating it, can seem a bit Victorian and fussy. This could not be further from the truth. Grace is the result of a body working smoothly. Grace is available to everyone; forget any associations with debutante balls or porcelain-painting classes. Cultivating it is simply a matter of becoming aware of how one is moving and correcting any quirks. The body is like an ecosystem—a knee slightly out of line means a thigh bone out of place, which means the hip is out of place. Surely you get the picture. The key to successful perambulation, ignored by too many, is so simple it's almost embarrassing. Ready? Here it is: Let your legs do the walking. Before you throw this book down in disgust, try this: Stand up and lift your leg from the thigh. Not from the hip, but lift from the top of the leg itself. Now take stock of the position you find yourself in. Are you leaning forward? Have you subtly popped the opposing hip out? Focus on bringing all those popping hips and raised shoulders back into line. You may want to try this in front of a mirror; often what feels aligned to us is not. We are so accustomed to being crooked, we don't know the difference! Now take a few steps while thinking of keeping the pelvis in bistro position, shoulders down and relaxed, and the head resting lightly on the neck. Heads have a habit of drifting forward, as if the hairline needs to arrive before the rest of you. Gently bring that anxious head back in line.

Changing one's posture, both walking and standing still, takes time. One wise suggestion is to check your posture every time you glance at the time. Do a mental sweep of your body. Shoulders down? Collarbone wide? Pelvis slightly tucked? It will soon be second nature.

Since most of us live in environments which require shoes and clothing, it is important to look out for the posture problems they cause. Shoes are the most obvious culprit, but they are not alone. Here are three foot and fashion faux pas to avoid:

1. Flip-Flop Waddle. Every summer, people all over celebrate the arrival of temperate weather by casting aside constricting winter shoes in favor of the flip-flop. Although we have discussed the flip-flop's appropriateness in various situations, we have not mentioned the very real problem of flip-flop–induced waddling. Now, some people are just prone to waddling—i.e., the extremely pregnant—but we are convinced that the unstructured nature of the flip-flop causes many other completely unnecessary cases. It happens like this: The feet, enjoying their freedom, are slowly allowed to turn out until they are no longer parallel. This gait not only looks ungainly from the front, it does terrible, terrible things to the view from the back. The legs are turned out from the hip joints, causing a general spreading and widening of the bottom. Take a look next time you are on the street. The most flat-bottomed among us tend to be those walking around with feet that are not parallel. Which came first, you might ask, the poorly placed feet or the pancake bottom? Does it matter? Why not be on the safe side and get those feet in line?

2. Elephant Walk. The undisputed queen of the shoe jungle is the high, high heel. We associate it with status and sex, and who doesn't occasionally want a little of those? The problem is, if you walk like a pachyderm, even Christian Louboutin can do very little for you. Just spend a few minutes any weekday on a major avenue in Manhattan at lunchtime. Out come legions of women in the most delicate of shoes, clump, clump, clumping their way to pick up a salad. The brutal truth is that if you wear high heels you must adjust your stride. Unfortunately, that fabulous, long, liberated stride you take in sneakers must not be performed in heels. Note that this is not a matter of skill. Plenty of women do take those huge strides in the most delicate of heels. The issue is not whether it *can* be done, we know from observing all those clumpers on the way to lunch that it is only too easy. The issue is that it should *not* be done. It looks terrible. Wearing high heels comes with responsibility. You want those taut calf muscles and a nicely angled bottom? You must pay the shoe piper by taking smaller steps. If you need to get somewhere fast in heels, make sure you have a pair of ballet flats or slim sneakers in your bag. This will save wear and tear on you *and* your heels. Once you arrive at your destination, slip behind a potted palm, catch your breath, and change your shoes. Emerge from behind the palm taking steps appropriate to your new footwear. Small ones.

3. The Terrible Tugs. Standing stock still in front of the mirror this morning, everything was just perfect. As long as you don't move too fast, the skirt will stay down and the top will stay up. That is, until you have to pick up your purse, or lean over, or take a sip of coffee. Then it's a viscious tug-of-war to keep yourself decent. Nothing ruins a nice time faster than clothing that demands more attention than your dinner companion. And how many times has a woman passed by whose pencil skirt, so demure on the hanger with its back slit to facilitate walking, is now revealing far more than its wearer seems to think? But she knows something is awry, and therefore has to stop every five paces or so to give it a good yank down. Clothing that must be tugged or yanked is either poorly constructed, doesn't fit, or both. No matter how beautiful, these pieces must be shunned or else you'll find yourself scuttling about looking and feeling uncomfortable. Nothing causes the shoulders to hunch faster than a top that seems on the brink of going AWOL. This is never chic or graceful.

THE WEIGHTLESS WALK

Now that we have covered some common walking gaffes, how about some suggestions to keep in mind for the next time you stand up? One of the easiest things to do is focus on keeping your step light. Before you take a step, try lifting one foot. Can you do it without shifting all your weight to your other leg and listing to one side? If not, stop to check that you are in bistro position and try again. A few attempts and you should be ready to go. As you set out walking lightly, allow your upper body to stay loose and relaxed—your legs are in charge now. The length of your stride should depend on the shoes you are wearing, as discussed above. This is by no means a push toward mincing, but it is important to narrow the stride as your heel height grows. The stride, regardless of footwear, should never be so long that you must allow your weight to fall forward with each step to "catch up" with the leading leg. Another way to think of this is that your hip bones should remain pointing forward as you stride. If your strides cause the bones to alternately stick out, your stride is too long.

We have all heard the advice that one should smile when feeling down because the very act of smiling, even if not spontaneous, causes the spirits to lift. The same can be said about how you hold yourself. Next time you are walking into a situation that makes you nervous, check your stride. Are you hunched and walking heavily? This will only add to your feeling of dread. Help yourself by keeping your head up and feet light. Not only will you feel better, you'll have a much faster start if you decide to bolt.

And now, moving from the inside out, we turn our attention to that most fabulous of organs, the skin.

SKIN

One hears how a particularly stylish person really "owns" a look. This means that they wear it naturally, no cringing or apologizing. How many people can say the same about their own skin? The time has come for you to really "own" that lovely dermis that covers you. Barring a gargantuan leap in the rate of scientific discovery, it's the only one you'll ever have.

Delighting in the dermis has nothing to do with being thin, smooth, and wrinkle-free. Before the scoffing begins, think back to a time you now regard as the apotheosis of your beauty. The twenty-four-year-old may think back to when she was fifteen and didn't really have hips. The sixty-year-old may remember forty fondly, but be assured, whether it was twenty years ago or two, they found something wrong about themselves then, as well. This is a tragic state of affairs, and although we may never escape completely, it is possible to view one's present self in a far rosier light.

Various cultural factors conspire to make the idea of being pleased with oneself suspicious. Perhaps it is the famous Protestant work ethic that has so shaped the West— the demand to constantly labor and constantly improve. (Or at least, to feel perpetually guilty that one isn't doing more.) We tell ourselves that we don't deserve loving treatment—not until we lose weight, fix our knobby knees, or get our arms waxed, freckles removed, breasts enlarged or reduced, eye color changed, or become a triathelete. Isn't that absurd? This is not about the rational assessment of one's plusses and minuses; this is mania.

There will always, *always* be something to fret over, and too often the fretting takes the place of actually taking care of oneself. Worrying that the leather of your handbag is tired is absolutely ridiculous when your own legs are looking leathery from lack of care. The fretting and guilt must stop and the place to begin is in the shower. The idea to evoke is one of the pleasant, agenda-free bath times of childhood. No need for heated rocks or other spa trappings.

All the process requires is the luxurious soap of your choosing and a mildly abrasive cloth. Something large enough to do the back is essential. If your idea of luxurious soap is Ivory because you love the smell, good for you. Begin by lathering up the cloth and starting with your toes. Work up the front of the body to the shoulder blades. Now, re-lather and start at your heels and work up the calves from the back side. Remember those vibrating-belt contraptions you occasionally saw '40s and '50s movie stars using? The idea was the vibrations toned the muscles while you simply stood there. Keep this in mind while scrubbing the backs of the thighs and bottom. Often we simply ignore the parts of ourselves we don't like, allowing them to fall even further into neglect. Scrub those ignored parts, metaphorically, back into the fold! After a rinse, step out and grab a towel, preferably a fluffy one. Slather on a lotion or body cream, again starting at the toes. Choose a cream because you love how it feels. Whether you shop at the drugstore or Neiman Marcus, there are so many interesting things to sniff and try. This is not the time to apply self-tanner or some other "treatment." Just relax. That felt good, didn't it?

YOUR VISAGE

Unlike, say, the elbows, one's face is constantly available for perusal. Store windows, butter knives, and bathroom mirrors all do their part to let us know how our kisser is looking at any given moment. This can be a blessing if it means discovering and removing the frisée from one's teeth before a meeting. It can also become oppressive.

What starts as mere looking often segues into scanning and searching. With narrowed eyes we hunt, first for incipient blemishes and then, as the years pass, for blemishes, fine lines, and suspicious pigmentation. The skin of our faces seems to be always threatening some fresh

hell. To placate it, we must offer supplication in the form of expensive creams, tonics, scrubs, and masques. What we suggest, as difficult as it seems, is to regard one's face less like an angry demi-god and more like, well, part of you. Practice looking in that magnifying mirror once a day and saying, "Hello, gorgeous." Until you get comfortable with the idea, you may want to do this in the privacy of your home.

Although regimens vary from woman to woman, there are a few basics that should not be ignored. First, everyone needs something to hold the hair off their face as they go through their morning and evening toilettes. Make yours whimsical; find the most outré clip or headband available. This is one of the few times that silk flowers or feathers are just perfect. There are very few chances in life to wear fake orange chrysanthemums on your head. Doing so while you wash your face is a lovely way to begin and end the day. It adds a fun, "Showgirl at the Copa" feeling to even the most mundane bathrooms. And headbands and clips are much more comfortable than pasties!*

As you go through your cleansing and exfoliating, please be gentle. From the first exposure to Noxzema onward, we often feel that if it doesn't hurt, it isn't working. Every dermis is different, but you would be amazed by how well the skin may respond to a bit less intervention. You should retire for the evening feeling soft and moisturized, not worn out from an epic struggle with fifteen different serums.

Unless those fifteen serums are fun to use and really work for you, how about trying the following program: Apply outré hair accessory; wash face while humming something from *Carmen*; dry with fluffy towel and apply moisturizer; pat on some eye cream while doing leg kicks. These are good for the bottom. Keep the pelvis in bistro position, point your toes, and focus on using the back of the legs to lift the leg directly behind you. Five on each side. Now, slick on a bit of lip balm, nothing too mentholated for evening. Brush your teeth and trot off to bed.

---

* Not that I've ever worn pasties. . .

In the morning, don't forget to apply your sunblock. There are now so many to choose from, and so many formulations available, there is no good excuse for skipping this step. Even if you have a darker skin tone and an eighty-year-old grandmother who looks forty, you still have no excuse. Perhaps you won't wrinkle, but you can still get blotchy. Use that SPF!

CROWNING GLORY

Take a look at the following syllogism:

Long hair is beautiful.
I have long hair.
Ergo, my hair is beautiful.

Does this resonate with you? Unless you can honestly say that your long hair is in great condition, with no hints of dry fuzziness, stringy sections, or last summer's highlights somewhere around your ears, you need to do some honest assessment. And we understand, it isn't easy, especially right now. American culture seems to be in the grip of a pagan cult that worships the flatiron. Every couple of seasons, the Velcro roller gets up there on the altar as well. This trend is hardly new. The most cursory research seems to suggest that the idea of the "crowning glory" dates back to the Old Testament. In the early usages, it's God being discussed, not Jessica Simpson, and it seems to be at least metaphorically a real crown, not a head of loose, beachy waves He's sporting. Still, it's an enduring idea and the time has come to question it. Ask not what you can do for your hair but . . . you know.

What can change your appearance more drastically than a new haircut? Isn't "Did you change your hair?" one of the questions people who secretly undergo plastic surgery always laugh about being asked? A chic, flattering haircut will further your quest for style more than anything else. We all know that hair is not a security blanket, and yet, many of us can't bear the thought of losing an inch, or deviating from the longish bob that's worked so well since 1992. How many women feel they couldn't live without their long hair, but wear it pulled back ninety percent of the time? It doesn't make sense to have hair that is not contributing to your overall look. The chic haircut, the haircut that says its owner has a point of view, will actually do far more than just contribute to a look, it can make the look. It is like having one fabulous accessory that is always with you and goes with anything. There is more to life than the longish bob or even long hair with layers. There are options beyond the pageboy or the pixie. In order to find them, though, you must seek out a stylist whose aesthetic sense you share. This does not mean somebody famous, just someone whom you trust and feel understands what you want. If you have gone to the same person for years and the spark is gone, explain that it's you, not them, and move on. Commit to a little exploration until you've found the stylist who can give you that Sophia Loren mane or Halle Berry crop or early Linda Evangelista look you've always wanted. Keep in mind, if you are in the midst of emotional upheaval, a new haircut may *seem* to be the perfect emblem of new-found liberation. However, what was chic and Joan Jett-esque at 6:00 P.M. may feel like Mr. Bean at 8:00 A.M. Perhaps you should allow the emotions to settle before committing to a big change. And remember, when it comes to the texture of your hair, make it work! Make sure your stylist understands your hair so you don't end up with a look that requires two extra hours every morning.

It is entirely worthwhile, by the way, to pay for the best hairdresser you can afford. You will, after all, be wearing what you pay for twenty-four hours a day.

The Blind Spot: Style is not just about clothes, nor is it something bestowed upon you if you are the correct shape or size. Style is about the way you hold yourself and move through the world. It is about paying attention to the details of you, which means embracing and taking full advantage of what you have to work with. Go forth, exfoliated and moisturized; be kind to your freckles; lose the ponytail; and position that pelvis. It will do far more for you than a new outfit.

SHOPPING

- ✓ black pants
- ✓ tailored suit
- ✓ pants
- stilettos
- ✓ necklace

Chapter Six

Preparing to Shop

The Lesson: After all that hard work in the closet, the time has come—almost—to shop. But before you do to the retail world what Alaric and his merry band of Visigoths did to Rome, it is key that you have in mind exactly what you are looking for. On the following pages you will find a list of looks and items that no closet should be without.

"I don't know how to shop in America."
—Diana Vreeland

THE TOP TEN

When it comes to a list like this, how tempting it is to rely on some old favorites: the strand of pearls, the little black dress, the crisp white button-down. We must, however, remember the rallying cry of the great Elsie de Wolfe, "Suitability, suitability, suitablity!" Elsie was talking about the decorating of interiors, not persons, but this advice is still apt. Pearls are beautiful, but are they the only piece of jewelry that imparts a quiet luxury? Not at all! And if you love a crisp button-down, and it flatters you, fabulous. But if a gorgeous cream cashmere shell better serves your torso, let that be your basic. The way we dress today means some new staples have come to the fore. With that in mind, take a look at this list:

1. The Trench-ish Coat. Like so many other enduring looks, the trench coat got its start in the armed services. As its name suggests, the coat was worn by British and French soldiers while fighting in the trenches of WWI.

A rather sad association, but the coat has also enjoyed enduring peacetime popularity. The traditional trench is double-breasted, belted, and often has a lining that can be removed for warmer weather wear. It is also rather long, hitting well below the knee. Today there are hundreds of trench spin-offs to choose from. The slightly shorter and narrower version is a foolproof way to finish a look. It gives jeans and a T-shirt some starch while keeping dressier looks from veering into fussy. And although Burberry still rides high in the trench world, there is no reason to feel that you must spend $1,200 just to get that plaid lining. Everybody now does something trench-ish, from Prada to H&M. Just remember that in a trench, as with all great design, form should follow function. Ask yourself if the coat provides adequate warmth for where you live, assuming you'll be wearing it from the early spring into late fall. Is it waterproof? Does it hit at a flattering spot on the leg? Is it too voluminous for your frame? Because even the world's most expensive plaid will be cold comfort if you look like your coat is swallowing you alive.

2. The Sweat Suit Alternative. There is something appealing about pretending we live lives that require prim little suits during the day and only the most challenging vintage Balenciaga by night. Even if that is your life, isn't it safe to assume that every so often you just need to be comfortable and enjoy some easy, unrestricted movement? For some of us, that might be almost every day, which makes the ease of the warm-up suit, running suit, or sweat suit all too seductive. The truth is, with a bit of investigative effort and imagination, you can find something just—or almost—as comfortable that will not tell the world that you may take a nap or hit the gym at any moment. For winter, try some cashmere pants, but instead of topping them with a matching cashmere hoodie, opt for a cardigan or sweater-coat that can work with all sorts of other pieces in your wardrobe. Why not try a cardigan with a crisp white tee, some black Capri pants, and a pair of skimmers? Or how about some slim black pants or dark jeans with a dark gray V-neck sweater? In warm weather, a great-fitting tee and some breezy linen pants will also do the trick. Maybe bring along a cashmere cardigan from your winter collection in case you encounter a blasting air conditioner. Soft cotton jersey pants should be avoided if one is going anywhere other than the yoga studio. Many a woman is walking around New York City right now with no idea that her pants not only reveal the shape of her bottom, but the shape her bottom is in. The only dimples that one should display in public should appear next to one's smile.

3. The Boot, the Pump, the Ballet Flat. Far, far more useful and interesting than an "it" bag, is a beautiful boot. Whether it is a traditional flat equestrian style or something with a dangerous heel, there are few fall and winter looks that don't work with a boot. A black boot is always useful, but a gorgeous brown pair is less expected. Dark greens can also be subtle and work with autumnal colors. Since strappy heels are now expected year-round,

a classic pump is a fresh alternative. Classic means a rather
delicate heel and a toe not so rounded as to evoke Minnie
Mouse. The ballet flat, which should have a place of

honor on every shoetree, can function like the sweetly
sophisticated older sister of the flip-flop. Flats are just as
comfortable, and, unlike the flip-flop, they work with
both the most casual looks and the most sophisticated.
Peeking out from under a wide-legged trouser or with a
skirt, ballet flats are feminine and graceful. They are also
perfect for travel. They are easy to get in and out of at
airport security checks and comfy for the flight. You'll
arrive in style while your plane-mates—many in velour
tracksuits and clunky sneakers—look ready for bed and/
or some jogging.

4. The Shapely Jacket and the Go-Anywhere Top.
In fall and winter, throwing on a beautifully fitting
blazer with jeans and boots is always chic. The combination of course, can take on almost unlimited shadings.
Something tweedy with an equestrian boot immediately
says Greenwich, Connecticut, while a shrunken, schoolboy
blazer and some motorcycle boots is all rock-and-roll.
A summer-weight version, unconstructed and unlined,

can work like a cardigan while imparting a much sharper look over dresses and tees. Although what goes under your jackets will vary with the seasons, it is imperative to have a store of tops that you know will work. These can be button-downs or thin cashmere or other knit. For summer, a great-fitting tank is essential. Happily, most are affordable enough that you can get them in a few colors.

5. Signature Jewelry. Perhaps we should split this category into two. First we have the piece that makes an impression and may satisfy all of one's accessorizing needs. In this category we place the incredible cocktail rings designed by Victoire de Castellane. Not only would it be foolish to try to wear any other jewelry with them, they cost so much, very few of us could afford anything else after purchasing one. So on one hand we have the "make a splash" signature piece, and on the other we have what we might call the "personal" signature piece. For some of us, maybe it is the classic strand of pearls, and if so, bully for you. But if you are not a pearl person—or if you are but want to find something new—there are so many other ways to go. How about a gorgeous sculptural cuff or some simple gold hoops à la Bridgitte Bardot? Keep in mind that size does not a signature piece make. The key to something becoming a signature piece is that it is always with you. Makes sense, doesn't it? We find there is something almost metaphysically pleasing about the idea: No matter what you wear, you have your special talisman/necklace/bracelet with you. Certainly we can all use a bit of continuity in this mixed-up world we live in, no?

Speaking of which, as you run from place to place, a striking watch is always appropriate and functional. Plus, it is so much more discreet to glance at your wrist rather than rummaging through your bag to look at your cell phone. There are so many styles, from the Tank—another classic that has martial beginnings—to the Tonneau; there is a shape and style for everyone. One note: Resist the urge to buy the watch—or bling—of the moment. There was a time when it seemed that Tiffany must have been handing out those sterling silver heart necklaces to every girl between the ages of eleven and twenty-one. God only knows what the traffic on Fifth Avenue would have been like if everybody decided to take Tiffany up on their request, stamped on each heart: "Please Return to Tiffany and Co." Bedlam! Legions of girls, some in their Juicy warm-ups, some in their cashmere pullovers and button-downs, trooping up the Avenue. . . . We shudder at the thought.

6. The Under Arsenal. This seems like common sense, but many a stylish outfit founders upon the rocks of poor foundation garments. The thong, although brilliant for removing the possibility of the dreaded VPL—visible panty line—does leave one rather exposed. Your under-wear drawer should be like a Boy Scout, always prepared. That simile is rather strange, but we trust you understand. The key to preparedness in the undergarment world can be summed up in one word: nude. Whatever shade you are nude, you *must* have panties and bras in tones that match *you* and will not show through sheer fabrics. Keep in mind that a top that seems perfectly opaque to you at

7 A.M. may, in the blazing sun of noon, be one step away from scandalous. Nude is always a safe bet, especially now that tissue-thin T-shirts and sweaters are so popular.

7. The Day Dresses. The very phrase evokes a bygone era, doesn't it? You know, bridge parties, rigid hairdos, and even more rigid social codes. Of course, both social codes and hairdos relax considerably after too many Manhattans at the country club. Happily for us, the day dress is still around and is perfectly hip and contemporary.

Every closet needs at least two for those mornings when separates pose way too much of a challenge. Although there are few things easier than throwing on a dress, something about them communicates that you have made an effort. This will lead to all sorts of nice treatment and may get you upgraded to a suite, or first class, or that table at Michael's you've always dreamed of. Your cool-weather dresses can be jazzed up with different tights or stockings. In summer, all you need are some streamlined leather sandals or ballet flats. Since our world has become increasingly casual, oftentimes a day dress can carry on through the evening. Yes, the classic advice for transitioning from day to evening is to change your jewelry, but does anyone want to do that anymore? Why not take advantage of the adornment nature has provided for you, the bust line? Many dresses, especially wrap dresses, can become dangerously low cut as you wear them. You can spend the day adjusting and retying, or instead simply wear a camisole under the dress. When evening arrives, remove the camisole and go forth.

8. The After-Five Look. The little black dress is, as we know, unbeatable. However, a gorgeous pair of tuxedo pants and a tank is another way to go. So often evening means "bigger," shinier fabrics; more skin; and a tighter fit; so there is something downright subversive—and chic —about going the other way.

What is most important is that if you received an invite to a cocktail party for that evening at 3:00 P.M.— terribly rude, but it happens—you have a look ready to go. Not just any look, but something you feel great in.

9. The New, Cheap, Terribly Trendy Item. Think of this as the pressure-release valve. An unavoidable part of style is discipline. But all that refusing in the name of elegance can feel restrictive. With the arrival of stores like H&M and Forever 21, you can buy a trendy item without having to stare mournfully at it four months later wondering why in God's name you spent four hundred dollars on a faux-fur chubby. Indulge occasionally in a twenty-dollar something or other. *If* you notice these items beginning to take over, though, you must be merciless in cutting yourself off. Cold turkey. This is not to suggest that all shopping done at H&M and its brethren is of this type. Just the outrageously of-the-moment items.

10. Denim. There was once a time before denim. Yes, it is true. Now we wear it everywhere, even to the opera and to religious ceremonies—well, *we* don't, but we've seen it! The basic denim wardrobe requires two fabulous pairs, one for dressing up and one for running around. If you wear jeans every day, of course, your collection should be larger. However, we feel that even the most ardent denim lover does not need more than ten pairs. Keep in mind that the average lifespan of a denim trend is twenty-four months. So please don't invest too heavily in the trend of the moment. Considering how expensive designer denim has become, it's better to fill out your wardrobe with fashion styles—stovepipe, cigarette, cropped—from lower-priced lines. And please, be kind to that flesh around your midsection. Forcing it to choose between popping over your waistband and trying to burst a button is cruel. Go a size up and cut the tags off if you must.

The Blind Spot: False economy. When shopping, the temptation to scrimp on more practical items is ever present. Please, please resist. Although the idea of spending more on a black cardigan, or high-quality-but-sedate undergarments, or another pair of gray flannel cuffed trousers may leave you cold, it is undoubtedly the right choice. By choosing to spend less on an item you wear all the time, you will ultimately end up spending more as your cheap item requires repairs or replacement. Instead, make your rallying cry "Buying well means buying once!"

Chapter Seven

Let's Go:
Shopping at Last!

The Lesson: We shop out of boredom, for release, for excitement, for a sense of achievement, for a sense of control over our unruly existences. And every so often, we shop because we need something to wear. Shopping did not always fulfill so many needs. It wasn't until the mid-nineteenth century that department stores sprang into being. Their tremendous success stemmed not only from their stock of goods conveniently housed under one roof but also from the space they provided for women to see and be seen in public at a time when a woman in a bar was an anomaly. Who wouldn't have wanted to shop? It sure beat being the ideal Victorian wife and mother, otherwise known as the Angel in the House. Borrrrring, and repressive! Why does this matter, you ask? Well, knowing why shopping occupies the place it does in our culture can only lead to your being a better, more astute shopper.

"Fashion can be bought. Style one must possess."
—Edna Woolman Chase

In this chapter we point out certain things to be aware of in each of the shopping venues that dominate the landscape today. It truly seems that shopping has never had a more prominent role in our culture. Once it was difficult to spend thousands of dollars while at home in your underwear, but no longer! There are so many places and ways to shop now, a fact which brings to the fore all sorts of problems.

The idea of mothers and daughters gathering around the same rounder of clothing is not new. The difference, it seems, is now mothers want to look like daughters, rather than the other way around. Although you and Mother may have shopped in the same store, chances are you would have found what you were looking for in different departments. The very fact that you existed and were old enough to shop meant your mother bypassed the "Young Miss" department. There was a time when children dreamed of the day they would have the trappings of adulthood for themselves. Those classic rites of passage have disappeared, though, like the gust of Shalimar following a woman into La Côte Basque. The rites were simple: For boys, historically, it was the switch to long pants; a move no longer so exciting, as Dad may wear shorts himself most of the time. For a girl it was a first pair of high heels, hardly an emblem of womanhood if Mom is usually in UGGs.

This former propriety in dressing and shopping meant there were stores that sold things that could truly ruffle some establishment feathers. Not anymore. The plight of the poor teenager working hard to display her ennui is quite serious. When little sister is in a baby Ramones T-shirt and Mom's laptop bag has a skull and crossbones on it, what's a kid to do? Once, thrift shops and small, niche stores catered to lovers of the outré. Today, chain stores sell the old emblems of dissatisfaction to people of all ages, alongside every possible temptation. Black nail polish, where is thy sting?

There is, of course, an upside to all this availability. With a little research and attention to detail you should always be able to find exactly what you need. The key is to shop wisely, which means—brace yourself—to shop less.

SHOPPING *PAR TOUT*: THE SUPERSTORES

Once there were places to shop where you could browse for hours, and places to buy things where you dashed in and out as quickly as possible. No doubt there are legions of people out there who would swear that they could spend hours at Pep Boys gazing at the motor oil and fingering the license-plate holders. We wish them luck. No matter how thrilling your local auto supply store, you probably enter with some notion of what you need, proceed to where it is located, peruse the four or five choices, and take your pick. The chances of being sidetracked by a fabulous car coat on your way to the spark plugs was once nil. That is no longer the case. Perhaps auto supply stores are still the exception, but someday we will see a car-loving designer break that barrier. Tom Ford for AutoZone racing suits or some such. On one hand, the fact that Costco has cashmere is good news. Who would have guessed that one day you could buy beef jerky in bulk right next to a baby-pink cashmere shell? It's a cross-species "use every part of the animal" philosophy!

On the other hand, it means that the line between living and consuming becomes increasingly blurred. And our finances have the scars to prove it.

We digress. However, living in a world where you can pick up a dress by a runway darling a few aisles from the Cheez-Its means that newer forms of shopping discretion must be used. Oh, how seductive the racks bearing those interesting names are! We all know that there is no such thing as a free peplum jacket, but look, this one is only $29! Yes, these bargains can be difficult to resist, but there are two questions that you *must* ask before tossing the jacket into your cart along with a popcorn popper and some juice boxes. One: Is the piece appropriate for the season it is being marketed for? Remember: Cotton and Christmas don't mix, no matter what your chic-but-cheap retailer tries to tell you. This rule of ours exists for a reason that has nothing to do with the fact that we have friends in the wool business. Life goes by quickly. We often repeat the same thing day after day: Wake up, work, go to sleep. We humans need variety! Because technology does a fine job of protecting us from the more extreme vagaries of our environment, you might ask, why not wear voile on Thanksgiving? Well, because then life is one long stretch of endless voile-wearing and, really, who wants that? What about the thrill of pulling out a gorgeous coat when the weather becomes crisp? Or the lovely lightness of a cotton blouse after a long winter of sweaters? The same goes for those who live in climates that don't change very much. Even Palm Beach needs to swap in lime green for black—or at least switch to lime green in duchess satin—

once in a while. It gives our world a little puff of that all-important variety and—this cannot be overstated—it means you get a break from some of your clothing, so you do not become desperately tired of everything you own.

The other argument against seasonally inappropriate fabrics is far more sober: In them you will look either under- or overdressed. No matter how polished the cotton, after October it should be put away. We are not talking about resortwear or the sheer cotton sweater in pewter worn with black ankle pants in Miami in January. We are talking about a sweater, obviously made of cotton and light in color, worn when there is snow on the ground. Or, a dress in fabric too light for the time of year and event. It may look great and it may be a bargain, but you wouldn't wear tartan in July, so don't wear linen in November.

Clothing in fabrics too light for the season in which it is being sold is now popping up all over the place, not just at the discount stores we mention. This requires restraint and knowledge on the part of the consumer. That thin cotton "holiday" dress will not only leave you feeling cold, but also looking ready for egg salad on a picnic blanket—not eggnog under mistletoe.

The second question to ask before buying a bargain is: Does this item perform as it should in both form and function? Let's pause for a word about form and function and this whole "democratization of design" business. Everyone with a good eye and a sensitive soul loves beauty. The ability to appreciate and feel joy when beholding something that speaks to you has nothing to do with your tax bracket. In fact, it sometimes seems that the sensitive soul may become a bit toughened on the way up to those higher brackets. That said, design for everybody is great—as long as nobody is being sold shoddy goods. Good design is about a marriage of form and function. Anybody who has gone a few rounds with an assemble-it-yourself Ikea bookcase can attest that it isn't the same experience as sipping a gimlet while your decorator makes sure the contractor is going to finish the built-ins on time. But, when it comes down to it, who cares?! If your books are well housed (the function), the thing looks good (the form), and it isn't threatening to collapse on you or your guests (basic standard of hospitality), bully for you *and* Ikea. Do not try to assemble the bookshelf while having a gimlet, though. Too dangerous.

Many pieces at box stores fulfill both the form and function requirements. Many others do not. The more complex a function—supporting your foot while it's balanced on a three-inch heel, for instance—the more likely that the item may compare unfavorably to its higher-priced brethren. The simpler the function—a stretchy camisole, a tote—the greater the chance for success. What too often happens with the more complex pieces is that you are getting the form with a seriously diminished function. It may be a leather jacket for $60, but if it is as stiff as an old boot—and not a nice, worn-in old boot—why would you want to wear it? Stock up on basics at these emporia, but be wary of pieces that seem too good to be true. And always, always try before you buy at the big bargain houses. Actually, always try before you buy, period. Sizing can be erratic and $20 is too much to spend if you are never going to wear it.

THE SHOPPING SAFARI

While most of the time we are firm believers in finding something good and sticking to it, for a moment we would like to suggest just the opposite. Forget everything you know—just for now—and strike out for the hinterlands. Now, if you are a dyed-in-the-tunic Eileen Fisher wearer, this might mean tolerating the music and throngs of teenagers for a look around Forever 21. Conversely, you Urban Outfitters fans might find a lovely pair of wide-legged, cuffed trousers on sale at Ann Taylor Loft. Since this is all about personal style, why should you be turned off—or on, but that's another story—by the marketing of a particular brand? This is about you, not who you're wearing. Of course you know that and are nodding sagely right now, but a reminder never hurts.

Keep the safari metaphor in mind. You are taking a trip through foreign lands—the locals may look different from you, and you might not want to trade iPods with them, but that is no reason not to enjoy the fruits of your adventurousness. You don't have to stay and you certainly don't have to buy anything, but you might be inspired, say, by the way an expensive shop puts together a look. A few stores later, you might be pleased to see something extremely similar in your price range. Don't limit yourself by gender or age, either. Smaller women have been finding fabulous jackets, sweaters, and button-downs from the boys' department for years.

DEPARTMENT STORES: KNOWING YOUR BUYER

The department store no longer has the hold it once did on our shopping lives. Mergers and market changes have done away with some of the greats—Bonwit Teller, you are not forgotten!—and the abundance of other shopping options have changed the field forever. That said, as long as malls need anchors, the department store will exist. Where else can you go when you have thirty minutes to buy both a cocktail dress *and* a juicer? And some shoes!

We all know that different stores cater to different customers. The smart shopper takes that one step further by acquainting herself with the buyer of her preferred lines. We are not suggesting you Google until you find out the buyer's name and invite her to a movie; only that you get a feel for her aesthetic at work.

Perhaps you've had the experience of seeing something in an ad or magazine and failed to find it at one store, though they carry the line, and then found it at another. While competing stores may share the same lines, what they don't share are the buyers. Each store employs buyers charged with picking the pieces of a particular line that best express the viewpoint of the particular store. That's why the Washington, D.C., Saks has different merchandise than the Fifth Avenue store. A great way to familiarize yourself with the different sensibilities at work is to visit, as we did, the same designer at two different stores. We chose Diane von Furstenberg. Selections from the line were at Saks and Neiman's. The Saks rounders were bursting with color and prints—the feeling was very wild weekend in Vegas. The selection at Neiman's, on the other hand, skewed toward meeting followed by dinner. Granted, it was still sexy—Diane Von Furstenburg simply is—but solids and more classic shapes dominated. If you are a wild-weekend-in-Vegas person, you know that you should proceed directly to Saks and spend the time you saved getting one more spray tan before heading to the airport.

Knowing your buyer also provides a bit of psychic armor against those items that you must avoid on your way to something suitable. Why is it that those items, the ones you know are no good for you, manage to appear so enticing on their hangers? Take, for instance, the clown cowl. On the hanger, perhaps even in the dressing room, it murmurs "drama, risk, excitement." Once home and paid for, it mocks you with its layers of fabric. Gone is the seductive whisper; in its place a sing-song of derision, something about "swags are for drapes." If you have faith that somewhere, far away from the clown cowl, your buyer will have something waiting that will not make fun of you, it may give you the strength to keep walking.

THE HIGH-END BOUTIQUE: *AVEZ-VOUS UN OUTLET?*

One of the few nice things about having less money than one would like is the discipline it fosters. Of course, it can also foster bitterness and rage—but let's look at the bright side! High-end boutiques offer wonderful inspiration, whether they carry a single designer's work or a beautifully edited collection of many. If you are attracted to the big names—Chanel, Burberry—they all have outlets these days. Before plunking down a huge sum, why not visit the boutique, note what you like, and then call the outlet? Nothing ventured, nothing gained—and you might save yourself a significant amount of money. If the outlet doesn't have it and you can't live another moment without snapping up whatever it is, go back to the boutique and buy with a clear conscience.

The individually owned boutique is often the most exciting and inspiring place to shop. They abound in New York City, and there is something beguiling about entering one person's vision, a complete sartorial world. If the owner is on target, each piece should fit, aesthetically speaking, with the others, creating a jewelry box of a universe. Add to the mix the person working in the boutique—often the owner—who perfectly epitomizes the look, and the magic is complete. You want it all! Never mind that you are an investment banker whose most daring piece is a slightly deeper than usual V-neck sweater and the store looks like Stevie Nicks's closet. You need those purple platform boots and the diaphanous maxi-dress and the beaded cape and the Mongolian lamb jacket . . . Wait! Step out of the store and take a deep breath. Perhaps this really is the first day of the rest of your wardrobe's life. Or perhaps it is just a momentary infatuation that will lead to a sorrowful head shaking in a few days' time. Why not hedge your bets and opt for one piece that both incorporates the elements you've become bewitched by and still works in your current wardrobe? Say no to the diaphanous maxi-dress and yes to a diaphanous blouse that will work under a jacket for the office.

THE OUTLET: EVER SO SLIGHTLY OFF

Once outlets sold exactly what you would expect: items from past seasons that didn't sell. Then came the great outlet explosion and the creation of the outlet mall. Suddenly it seemed every store had an outlet. Seeing a new opportunity, companies started manufacturing clothing specifically for their outlet stores. This could just be us, but knowing that dampens the thrill a bit. Isn't part of the appeal imagining the jacket you've just snapped up at Woodbury Commons—the premier, if there is such a thing, outlet mall an hour from New York City—once hung on a rack on Fifth Avenue? One can't howl over the kill with the same kind of lust knowing the item was born to be a bargain. Then again, if the jacket fits beautifully and the fabric is of an appropriate quality, howl away.

Often items created exclusively for an outlet are sized differently. Not a huge difference, but if you are a committed lover of the—entirely imaginary—Medea pant at a particular store, try on the outlet Medeas before buying an armload. Usually the outlet-specific items are made from different textiles, which can affect the way they fit.

We are of two minds on outlet shopping. It is possible to find great deals on pieces that a line makes year after year. This is surgical-strike outlet shopping. You know what you want, you call ahead, receive confirmation, and swoop in. The second, more dangerous form of outlet shopping is the open-minded browsing approach. This involves, as you might imagine, going from store to store and seeing if anything catches your fancy. Why is this dangerous? Well, the idea of a sale seems to short-circuit the brain's discernment apparatus. "These andirons are seventy-five percent off! I've got to get them." That's fine, until you get them home and remember you don't have a fireplace. The old adage is that you should never buy something on sale that you wouldn't buy at full price. A truer adage has never been uttered, but the outlet shopping experience seems to be predicated on the fact that people love to ignore an old adage. Remain strong and the outlet experience can work for you. Give in and you'll simply have more to give away on the next closet cleaning.

VINTAGE: SMELLY, EXPENSIVE, AND JUST RIGHT

Other than real estate, few things illicit such a fervent desire to go back in time and buy like vintage clothing. There seem to always be smug people who can say, "Oh, this? Yes, it's Dior, but I got it for $6.35 in a thrift store in Canton, Ohio. Of course that was fifteen years ago . . ."

Once "vintage" had a more specific meaning than it does today. Generally speaking, it meant something at least twenty-five years old, usually older. It was the turf of the eccentric and bohemian. The idea of wearing old clothes was simply not mainstream. Certain groups—fans of rockabilly music for instance—made vintage clothing a large part of their culture, but it wasn't until the early '90s and the ascendancy of grunge that vintage really hit the mainstream. Kurt Cobain may have done more for the cardigan sweater than anyone since Fred Rogers. The look actively rejected the shiny and new in favor of the ratty and recycled. Until the fashion world caught up, the only place to get the look—assuming your grandparents hadn't thoughtfully saved a choice selection of beat-up togs for you—was the thrift or vintage store. Grunge as a fashion moment passed, but the doors of the vintage clothing shops had been thrown open, never to close. Subsequent trends meant interest in vintage has waxed and waned, but just barely. It has successfully permeated the red carpet, and instead of suggesting eccentricity, now suggests taste, a good eye, and subtlety.

Back to the intense regret that you didn't buy that $15 YSL *le smoking* when you had the chance. The world at large is now so entirely aware of the worth of vintage clothing that most of the affordable things one finds today were home-sewn. You can find boutiques of gorgeous, beautifully edited collections of vintage designer clothing, of course, but what you will not find there is a bargain. Does this mean that you should despair of ever finding some hidden treasure? No, but you may have to adjust your idea of "treasure." Although vintage clothing often encourages a desire for the zany, the classic pieces are your best bet. Camel hair coats, Fair Isle sweaters, and printed summer skirts are looks that do not date. You want the clothing to delicately allude to another era, not shout that you are recreating the look your Great-Aunt Mildred wore to the USO dance where she met your Great-Uncle Fritz. Also be wary of the nostalgic mist that may dim your eyesight and trick you into thinking a beaded cardigan or net swimsuit cover-up is a good purchase. That is, of course, if you live a life that does not require a heavily beaded sweater or net cover-up. According to the laws of vintage shopping, if you do lead such a life you will be inexorably drawn to the faux-fur vests instead.

Since designers today borrow liberally from the looks of even the immediate past, buying vintage can be an excellent way to wear a trend without investing too much. However, often the "real thing" just doesn't look like the newfangled version when you try it on. First, as we've discussed, sizing has changed. Second, what proportions are appealing to the eye change with time as well. Third, since any vintage shop typically has only one of the item you are trying on, the odds of it fitting you well are slim. Beware of the desire to be dishonest with yourself. If you find yourself saying, "I think these sleeves are long enough," they aren't. With a rueful sigh, put the piece back on the rack and move on. When you do find something, promise us you will always wash or dry clean your vintage purchase before wearing.

THE INTERNET: ALL SHOPPING, ALL THE TIME

The idea of ordering clothing sight unseen is not new; catalogues have been offering the opportunity for eons. However, for sheer breadth and accessibility, the Internet has no equal. It has changed every category in this chapter and the way we all shop. As customer service in many stores has become a rarity, the human-free shopping provided by the Internet grows ever more appealing. There are a few rules which must be observed in order to make returning whatever just arrived a bit less likely.

Be aware of pinning. This is a shopping rule that should always be followed, since many brick-and-mortar stores are guilty of the exact same thing. Here's how it goes: You see a boat-neck sweater online—or in a window—that hugs the curves of the form it is on. Perfect! Just what you want to go with your fuller skirts. You click and it's yours. After a few days of happy anticipation your sweater arrives, and it's a flour sack. Yes, it's the same sweater but some crafty merchandiser realized that no one would want such a shapeless rag so, using binder clips or some other such device, pulled the excess fabric taut on the mannequin and snapped the picture. There are a couple of ways to get around devious pinning. One, if you are shopping in a store, compare the pieces in the window to the same pieces on a hanger. If they look curvy and fitted in the window and boxy and loose on the hanger, you are among pinners. Keep this in mind the next time you shop in this store or its online counterpart!

If you are shopping online, pay extremely close attention to the description of the fabric included with the item. This often indicates the snugness of the fit. By doing a little research in your own closet you can gauge how much 5 percent spandex in a pair of jeans will affect the fit. Then apply the knowledge to your online endeavors.

INSTANT GRATIFICATION: H&M

Oh, how these stores have changed the way we shop! What Ikea did for furniture, H&M has done for clothing. Namely, offering forward-looking design at extremely low prices. After becoming a mainstay in Europe, the chain is slowly spreading across the US. Those Swedes must love a bargain! We are continually, *continually* surprised by how much good stuff is available for so little money at these places. Now, is this a paradise of uncrowded peaceful browsing in which every item is beautifully constructed? No, it is bedlam, with racks so jammed that it is difficult to see what is actually on them. Nor will you find the same things if you decide a week later to go back for that sweater you regret not buying. It will be replaced by swimsuits, or parkas, or shiny tunics. H&M reduces shopping to its most instinctual: you hunt, you stalk, you pounce. All that hunting and pouncing can lead to your system becoming absolutely flooded with adrenaline. Once the heart starts pounding, judgment can be blurred, and the next thing you know you are the proud owner of a washed silk tube-topped jumpsuit or three. The key to shopping these bargain Ngorongoro Craters is to have a plan. Let us stay with our crater metaphor for a moment. The Ngorongoro, by the way, is in Tanzania, adjacent to the Serengeti. All sorts of animals live in or pass through the crater: It is a busy place, much like H&M. The question you must ask yourself as you prepare to shop is this: Am I an ungulate or a big cat? We, personally, use the big cat approach. It favors speed and focus. That way you'll have made your purchases—or at least be in line—by the time your nerves start to go from all the stimulation. Perhaps you are of a calmer temperament, more of a wildebeest than a cheetah. The wildebeest takes longer to shop than the cheetah, but her chances of finding something great are higher since she can patiently paw through the piles. Wildebeests have hooves, not paws, but you understand . . . .

Really, there are so many places to shop and so much merchandise available that the most important part of your expedition should take place before you leave home. The salient question to ask is: "Why am I shopping today?" This should not be an exercise in self-mortification, simply a little question-and-answer with the self. Maybe you've had an absolutely infuriating week at work and need to blow off some of that nervous energy. A walk will do you good. Promise yourself that you will pick out a treat—yes, you've made it through a bad week, you deserve it. The key is to make the treat something that will make you happy as you finish the day browsing, without stressing your budget or adding another piece of clothing/pair of shoes/handbag to your stuffed closet. That can only lead to more nervous energy followed by more shopping and . . . you see the pattern. Opt for something you can use up and throw out, a luxurious body cream or new bath product. Maybe some cosmetics? A new lip color can be a tonic for the soul. The Calvinists out there may shudder at such a shallow thought, but even another $25 lipstick is a better deal than a $250 sweater bought out of frustration, boredom, or unhappiness.

The Blind Spot: This whole "you deserve it, lip gloss is a tonic for the soul" business does not mean that you should consider a weekly lip gloss bill in the three figures appropriate. If you do find that you are constantly tempted to shop for emotional release, take a harder look at what is making you feel stressed. Problems that seem absolutely insurmountable can often be quickly—or at the least, more effectively—surmounted than you might guess. Next time you feel the "must-spend money mania" coming on, invite someone you trust to do the shopping with you. Use the opportunity to talk about what is bothering you. Afterward, you may very well feel satisfied with going home and trying on the clothes—and lip glosses—you already own.

Chapter Eight

Accessories: Say No to the "It" Bag

The Lesson: Simple enhancement or opportunity for unchecked theatricality? In the last ten years accessories have made a stunning return to the fashion stage. Now toddlers covet their mother's Manolos and small dogs refuse to be carried in anything that didn't cost their mistresses an arm and a leg. This is telling since animals and children are attracted to big, sparkly things and that's exactly what many of today's more popular accessories are: Too big, too shiny. You wouldn't let your Yorkie select your outfit, presumably, so why should Mr. Squeaks dictate your choice in bags?

"I never met a handbag I didn't like."
—A trend-crazed colleague

Enough silliness. The old saw about proper accessorizing is that you should remove one item before going out. This suggests that you have more than one item on, which raises its own troubling questions. Furthermore, with the advent of layered necklaces—which often look fabulous—this piece of advice should be retired. Where so many people run into trouble is that they look like they just played an exhausting round of Supermarket Sweep on the Bloomingdales accessories floor. Every item screams out its provenance, from the initials on the bag to the initials on the sunglasses to the initials on the driving mocs. You can probably name the perfume as she stomps by, too. This is not so much style as armor—"Look!" these items plead. "My owner has money and receives the same magazines you do!" Why not carry a plastic bag from the supermarket and simply tape your credit card statement to it? It saves wear and tear on the items but still gets the message across!

THE HANDBAG

Depending on where you live, this item might be known to you as a purse or pocketbook. It is also the backbone of many designers' businesses today. Purses and perfume allow a wider range of customers to bask in the particular glow of their chosen house. We'll return to perfume later. Bags are large—compared to a watch or glasses—and we wear them every day. This makes them the perfect status symbol. A $400 bra is lovely, but difficult to exhibit to a large audience without a whole passel of other issues. The predominance of the bag in the status sweepstakes means we must describe it with special language. May we propose a critical reading of the handbag? Yes, we will borrow some words you'll remember from high school English class to allow you to make sure that your bag is not *Moll Flanders* if you're a Bergdorf Blonde. Consider the following examples:

Tone: This is the general mood that you and your clothing set. For instance, you are twenty, home from college for Thanksgiving, and meeting your high school nemesis, Ruthie, at the local Starbucks. You and Ruthie are friends now, but you've taken care to blow dry your hair extra straight. Take that, Ruthie!

Diction: The items you choose to create the above-mentioned mood. Since it is Starbucks and the middle of the day, you opt for pink velour sweatpants and a coordinated boat-neck T-shirt. These items are casual, informal. You are, however, a woman of great sophistication, so you grab your huge Louis Vuitton Speedy before applying lip gloss and heading out the door.

Denotation of the bag: What is the bag really? Well, it's brown leather, has handles and a zipper. It holds things. That is not, however, what will make Ruthie jealous. Rather, that's the . . .

Connotation of the bag: Wealth, glamour, founded in 1854, advertised by J.Lo and carried by Jessica. You get the idea. Even frumpy Ruthie recognizes those letters.

So, what's wrong with this picture? Your diction is clashing with your tone, young lady. Yes, we said it. Your tone is extremely casual, you and your clothes are going for coffee at the mall. However, your bag is ready to go to a meeting in Paris. But isn't that a perfect illustration of the whole high/low thing that everybody is always talking about? No, it is not. In this case, the disparity is too large for the look to work. Instead of your bag and clothing creating harmony, the bag sticks out like an extremely expensive sore thumb. If the bag is a knockoff, it will stand out like a sore thumb whose pigment is slightly off and Ruthie will no doubt be able to spot it. Happily, a tone/diction clash is easy to fix. The first method involves grabbing another bag, perhaps that LeSportsac you have hanging on the back of your door; nice casual nylon that works with your knock-around clothes. The second method is the one we endorse. Trade in the sweatpants for some well-fitted jeans—neither painfully tight nor baggy, and please trade the tee for a thin boat-neck sweater and the sneakers for some ballet flats. You've upped the level of diction enough that the bag no longer looks out of place.

CHOOSING A BAG

Purchasing a bag should be approached like purchasing a pet. You must assess how much space you have, how much maintenance can you handle, and always be aware that a good bag will be with you for many, many years. If you have limited space in your closet or bank account, the key is, of course, to find that one absolutely perfect bag that works with everything, from beach picnic to midnight supper after a riotous black-tie party in honor of a dashing Polish aristocrat. As you can imagine, this is nigh impossible. You will need a small selection of bags that can take you through every imaginable situation. Even walking the aristocrat's dog while carrying a laptop. Truthfully, that might require two bags.

First let us talk about some very basic ideas to keep in mind about a bag's styling. The less structure the bag has, the less formal it is. Conversely, a bag that has a frame is more formal. How can one tell if it has a frame? One way is to put the bag down. Can it stand up on its own? Often bags with frames inside come with feet, or something to keep the bag from sitting directly on the floor. These bags have a more tailored, trim appearance. This is not the bag to carry if everything you own works well with Birkenstocks—even the metallic or patent leather ones. The Birks lover will be better served by a slouchy style, like a hobo bag. Although slouchy bags can be just as expensive and ornamented with just as many buckles and rabbits' feet, the style generally feels younger and less formal.

THE WORKHORSE

This is the bag that can go to the office with you every day. It should be large enough to hold what you need to transport without straining its seams or losing its shape. These bags tend—since many of us like to carry quite a bit—to be larger. That is not, in itself, a problem. However, two rules must be observed. One, the bag should work with your proportions. If you are five feet tall, a huge bag slung over your shoulder or arm will absolutely overwhelm you. Second, just because you are tall, don't think you can get away with passing off a small piece of luggage as a purse. There is a line that is almost impossible to identify between "large purse" and "small carry-on." You know it when you see it, though, we assure you. If you have your doubts, opt for a size down. Often the issue isn't so much size as design when it comes to looking luggage-esque. Duffel shapes are particularly vulnerable to this confusion.

When shopping for a workhorse, look for a strap large enough to distribute the weight of the bag comfortably. A large bag with a thin, single strap can be hell on the shoulder or arm. The pain will cause you to hunch, which will throw off your posture, which will ruin everything, so make sure the bag is well engineered before you buy.

Since this bag will be serving multiple functions and outfits, make sure that any fittings and embellishments are the right tone. In other words, if you are a die-hard gold fan, a bag with a huge silver clasp, silver zipper, and a million silver grommets is not a good choice.

This raises the issue of color. The best-case scenario is that you have one workhorse that goes with black and cool-toned shoes, and another that works with browns and warmer tones. If one color dominates your wardrobe, spend the money on that bag and find something great looking, but cheaper, for your second bag.

Before you suggest that this is impossible, let us share

an anecdote: We were in a meeting with an extremely stylish young woman. Her blond bob was glinting as we said good-bye and she swung her zippered and pocketed bag onto her shoulder. When she was complimented on the bag, she replied with a wry smile and two words: "Thanks, Target!" Was it made of the softest leather of virgin cows raised solely on honeysuckle-scented grass? Not at all. Did it pretend to be a $1,500 bag that it wasn't? No, it wore its inspiration lightly. Did it look great and get the job done? Absolutely.

THE SUMMER BAG

Although many a workhorse can go almost year round, the lightest of summer clothes—especially when on vacation or out of the city—require a lighter bag. This is the time for woven straws, raffia, or even canvas. A straw or canvas bag that has some structure and dressier detail can go to the beach and the office. Mind you, when we say go to the beach, we mean for a walk. For actually carrying towels and Bain de Soleil, dive in and get something cheap and cheerful. It's summer!

THE EVENING CLUTCH

Few things cause anxiety like the realization that the one evening bag you bought for prom doesn't work with the vintage Grès gown you are currently wearing. Or that the minaudière you have that looks like a sparkly eggplant clashes with your cocktail dress. To always be on the safe side, buy a simple black evening clutch. There are a million variations to be had, of course, but keep in mind you want this to go with all your formal and semi-formal wear, not just with what you are wearing that evening. If you'd like to experiment a bit, an evening bag is an excellent item to look for in vintage shops.

SHOES

Oh, where to begin? We recently visited the grande dame of tri-state area malls, the Mall at Short Hills in Short Hills, New Jersey. Notice the structure of the name; under no circumstances should it be called the Short Hills Mall. We say this half in jest, but even the most mild-mannered resident of the area will correct you. We circulated quietly through the Neiman Marcus shoe salon, furtively glancing at the shoppers in an attempt to gauge their shoe-buying habits. We can now confidently say this: People are willing to spend an ungodly amount of money on shoes. We could have stayed home and watched reruns of *Sex and the City* and come to the same conclusion, but we enjoy fieldwork. Shoe buying is intensely personal; one woman's walking shoe is another woman's high heel. We were once at dinner with a woman who slipped out of her Prada heels after the meal and into a pair of patent leather Gucci kitten-heeled sandals for the walk home. *Chacun à son goût,* and to each their own podiatrist's bill. Regardless of taste and budget, every closet should have the following:

1. Two pairs of boots—one dressy, one casual.
2. Flats that can go to the office, but work with jeans as well.
3. One pair of daring, dress-anything-up evening shoes.

THE PREVALENCE OF THE PASHMINA

For many years, scarves and wraps were not as popular with American women as with their European counterparts. Of course people wore them, but not everyone was slinging something jaunty around their necks every day. Then came the great pashmina boom of the '90s. Suddenly they were everywhere, and with them came whispers of secret "special" stashes made from illegally harvested goat-hair fiber. Evidently this harvesting did the goats absolutely no good and was banned. Today pashminas are ubiquitous. They can be purchased on Seventh Avenue, literally right next to the guy selling sugared peanuts. You can get them online or at any department store, and a casual survey suggests that many, many women have. The quality varies tremendously and, generally speaking, proximity to sugared peanuts is inversely proportional to quality. We love a pashmina and feel that it is a wonderful way to add interest to a winter coat. Yes, they've gone from a trend to a staple, but there are a few rules that should be observed.

First, neutral, softer colors are the best choices. We've found that they look good even if they are not of fantastic quality and will be the most versatile. Since this is going around your neck, you don't want a lurid color fighting with your complexion. The richer and deeper your skin tones, the richer and deeper your wrap can be while remaining neutral. Spice shades can be especially flattering to deeper complexions. Pale folk may want to experiment with ivories, taupe, and camel. The desired effect is one of quiet luxury; a soft, sensuous drape of fabric framing the face.

Second, if you plan on wearing a light-color pashmina with a dark coat or sweater, do a test at home to see if you are going to have lint problems. If so, be prepared with a small lint brush in your bag. In fact, always have a small lint brush in your bag.

Third, if you are planning on wearing your pashmina as a wrap for your shoulders, especially to a dressy event, invest in the best quality you can. The lesser quality versions may look great around the neck but appear flimsy when draped over the shoulders. Always make sure that you are draping artfully. You do not want to appear to have thrown a tablecloth over your shoulders. A gentle knot in front and some arranging of folds should do the trick.

The fourth and final pashmina rule involves proportion. Make sure that it is long enough to comfortably knot around your neck, with plenty of fabric left over. There is something melancholy about fringe hitting the breastbone. It looks as if the owner forgot about her scarf in the dryer. Just as in entertaining, you want generosity without over-the-top super-abundance. In this case, over-the-top super-abundance occurs when the pashmina is so large that, if knotted under the neck, the wearer cannot look down at her shoes. That situation is impractical and unnecessary.

A quick note on lightweight versions. The pashmina as winter staple has whet the appetite for year-round neck-bourne textiles. This is another market once cornered by European university students. While there is nothing wrong with a crinkled cotton version, be aware that the look is extremely casual. At its best it says insouciant urban nomad: You can use your scarf for an impromptu picnic blanket if the mood strikes. At worst, it suggests you just left the hostel.

SILK SCARVES

King of this category is the Hermès scarf. Available in a multitude of patterns and colors, this is a scarf that comes with connotations of wealth and luxury. That combo, though infinitely popular, can read a bit staid. The silk scarf is a piece that definitely benefits from a "This old thing?" approach. You know, running to catch the train, you dash out of the house and knot it carelessly around your neck. You arrive looking flushed and fabulous. Although women of any age can pull off a scarf, we once saw a girl of twelve or thirteen wearing a Hermès scarf as a headband. Her black hair was perfectly combed and she was wearing large dark glasses. She looked like she was about to trick-or-treat as a tiny Gloria Guinness. Assuming that you are not twelve, experiment with a scarf.

PERFUME

There is no accessory greater, or more intimate, than scent. Before we begin to discuss the power of perfume, let us first outline a few useful terms. Keep in mind that you could spend years learning about scents and the chemical structures that compose them. This is just a very brief sketch to help you as you begin your study.

Notes

These are the different elements that one can smell in a fragrance. Most perfumes are composed of top notes, what you smell as soon as the perfume is applied, followed by middle notes, then anchored by base notes. These base notes often give the impression of warmth and help the scent to last. As the scent evolves after application, it is said to "drydown."

When sniffing, for instance, a scent called Chat Sur L'herbe you might say, "I'm getting distinct notes of patchouli, fruit, and kitten fur." Since scent and our responses to them are intensely personal, your best friend might say of the same scent, "I get the patchouli note, but also a maple syrup note." An hour later when you both sniff, she might add, "But the drydown is musk and Abba Zabba notes."

Talking about perfume is very similar to discussing wine—the more vocabulary you have, the more fully you can articulate how you feel about the juice. One way to educate your nose is to start sniffing everything around you. People have far, far stranger habits, so if anyone looks at you askance, politely tell them that you are expanding your olfactory horizons. As you crack open a new hardback book, breathe deeply. It smells different from a book that's been on your shelf for years, doesn't it? Before you begin eating pad thai, think about the crisp lime juice and the sweetness of the tamarind paste and the salty tang of fish sauce. Not only will your nose benefit, you will enjoy your take-out far more. Once you begin sniffing you will be able to better identify how certain scents make you feel. Perhaps the smell of suede is comforting because of a loved one's jacket or the smell of oranges stresses you out because it reminds you of the holidays and it's already October and you haven't even begun to start shopping and . . . you get the picture.

We are all exposed to our culture's idea of what smells "good." Part of becoming an accomplished sniffer is learning to transcend those barriers. No need to start sniffing the neighbors' garbage, but do keep an open mind. Many people admit to liking "strange" smells, like a whiff of road tar or a hint of gasoline. Certainly you wouldn't want a tar-scented candle, but the occasional whiff has a certain piquancy. Many fragrances contain notes that add a bit of a jolt, the equivalent of a whiff of gasoline. Some, like Comme des Garçons' Odeur 53, are composed of a series of jolts: notes of nail polish, burnt rubber, and copy-machine toner. Together, they smell pleasant, synthetic, and clean.

Scent Families

Perfumes can be broken down into four extremely broad categories. The first category we will discuss is the Chypre. Oak moss, leather, and wood are the backbone of many Chypres, along with a fruit note or a floral note. The fruity Chypre par excellence is Guerlain's grand classic Mitsouko with its luscious peach note. An example of a lovely floral Chypre is Agent Provocateur. In its case, the floral note is rose. To the uninitiated, Chypres may smell "old" upon first sniff. That is because this family has been pushed aside by their far more accessible cousins, the fruity Florals. Spend some time with the Chypres, though, and you will be won over. They have character—and that's something we all need. For those of you who like wit with your scent, remember that Dorothy Parker was famous for dousing herself with the 1917 Chypre that started it all, Chypre by François Coty.

The Chypres' next-door neighbors are the Orientals. These are the scents that are usually described as spicy and warm. Notes like amber, musk, vanilla, balsam, and tonka bean often play large roles and give the scents a languorous feel. Some Orientals are extremely rich and potent, like Yves Saint Laurent's '70s classic Opium, while others are austere and redolent of incense, like L'Artisan Parfumeur's Passage d'Enfer. Still others seem almost edible or gourmand, like Thierry Mugler's Angel or another Guerlain classic, Shalimar.

Sunning themselves in the orchard out back is the Citrus family. Light and refreshing, this family makes up many eau de colognes and often socializes with herbs and spices. These scents can be light and stimulating, like 4711's Eau de Cologne No. 4711, or spicier, like Acqua di Parma's Colonia Assoluta. Although almost any fragrance can be worn by a man or a woman, Citruses are especially flexible.

And finally we have the Florals. A huge, sprawling family that encompasses everything from the shyest violet *soliflore*—a scent composed of a single floral note—to the lush and heady jasmine, rose, and ylang-ylang of Jean Patou's Joy. Some Florals are lighthearted and playful, seeming to jump around and scream, "Youth!" Others are world-weary and ready for another round of gimlets.

What to Wear

Just because you happen to be ready for another round of gimlets does not mean that you must wear a fragrance that evokes the same. Ask any perfume aficionado, and they will tell you that just as the marketing of a fragrance to a particular gender is nothing more than marketing—so are suggestions that something might be "too young" or "too old." We will concede that the twelve-year-old we mentioned in her Hermès scarf might have been compounding the problem if she added a healthy spritz of the 1981 Oriental blockbuster Must de Cartier. However, barring babies getting into the benzoin, your fragrance choice should not be dictated by your age.

It should, however, be dictated by the constraints of common courtesy. Always apply with a light hand if you are leaving the house. Keep in mind that the nose becomes accustomed to something it is constantly exposed to.

While you may think you are in need of a touch-up spritz, the people breathing through their mouths at the next table may find you quite potent.

Seasonal Scents

Depending on where you live, this may not be an issue. Furthermore, there is no hard-and-fast rule that all light Florals must be dropped, along with your white shoes, on Labor Day in favor of things that smell like black pepper, gingerbread, and pine trees. However, if you live in a place like New York City, where the summer sun beats mercilessly down through the humid air, you may not always feel like wearing Chanel Bois des Iles. On a sticky August day, a refreshing splash of Hermès Eau d'Orange Verte will hit the spot. Think of it as an icy glass of lemonade versus a steaming glass of mulled wine. Fast forward six months as you walk down the same street you walked down in August, but it is now freezing and absolutely covered in snow. That warm, rich Bois des Iles will cling beautifully to your scarf and your skin, providing a glow on a frigid day. Would you want lemonade now? Of course not! Well, we wouldn't, but perhaps you just have an unquenchable thirst for lemonade. By all means—drink it year round. Our one request would be that you mulled wine lovers apply very sparingly in the summer, especially if you plan to sit next to us on the subway.

The Blind Spot: From teen warblers to tennis players, to star of French cinema Alain Delon, it seems that everybody has a perfume with their name on it. So how can a fragrance survive in such a crowded marketplace? The same way breakfast cereals and snow shoes are sold: through marketing! Often our first point of contact with a fragrance is through an ad. We see a photo in a magazine or read the glowing advance press and become convinced that this is the scent for us. By 3:00 P.M. on the day Parsons graduate Narciso Rodriguez launched his eponymous fragrance at Saks, every stairwell, elevator, and hallway at the Department of Fashion Design was lightly perfumed with it. The student body had obviously visited Saks on their lunch break. Luckily for us, Narciso's scent is captivating and deserving of its popularity. However, always sniff for yourself no matter how captivating the photo or gushing the review. Of course, this also works the other way: You might be surprised how much you enjoy something you heard worrisome things about before sniffing it out for yourself. Just as you never have to tell anyone what size you bought those pants in, you need never reveal that your perfume came adorned with a little puff of marabou.

Chapter Nine

Not Your Everyday Occasion

The Lesson: Remember when you were a child and had party clothes? Those carefree days of white anklets and patent leather Mary Janes? With adulthood, one gains so much—as lovely as a Shirley Temple may be, a cabernet works better with dinner—but the ease of dressing for festive events is gone forever. Just like your baby fat. Now you may have adult fat, but that's not the focus of this chapter. Returning a bit of that childish ease to dressing for the out-of-the-ordinary event is what we'd like to do. With a bit of foresight, no invitation—grand or grimy—will throw you.

"You may well ask what 'formal' means in a world where such a thing exists as—Miss Manners shudders but takes your word for it—a pink dinner jacket."
—Judith Martin, author of the
"Miss Manners" newspaper column

Today, our point of reference for glamorous dressing is watching our favorite celebrities get gussied up and parade down the red indoor/outdoor carpet. "Not me," some may sniff. "My point of reference for glamorous dressing is John Singer Sargent." Fine for you, but the rest of us will be tuning in for the Emmy arrivals. That said, watching all that parading of famous frippery begins to warp our idea of what glamour unconnected to Nielsen ratings should look like. We believe that it has fostered a "more is more" attitude. After growing up watching J.Lo, why would a discerning child want to wear anything but Cavalli for her first communion?

We would like to see a return to a subtler form of glamour, a less sparkly form of glamour. Think of it as less Marilyn, more Lauren Bacall.

DECODING INVITATIONS

Once people lived by a code. Whether it involved Arthurian feats of bravery followed by some balladry, or *Ved forsigtighet og bestandighet**, you can bet that the Knights of the Round Table or King Frederick V of Norway always knew exactly what to wear to cocktails. Today things are not so simple. It's still possible to get a comprehensive guide to etiquette that explains exactly what to wear when, but there's a good chance that you'll be the only one at the party who's read it. If you are the type who will feel comfortable in your brogues, fedora, and traditional peacock-feather collar because that is simply the correct costume for a Yorkshire hunting party in mid-April, lovely. If, however, you notice everyone else is in jeans and cashmere and begin to feel a twinge,

---

* The king who reigned over Denmark and Norway from 1746 to 1766 employed this phrase as his motto. It means "By caution and consistency." This seems like an excellent idea in matters political as well as sartorial.

being correct may ultimately be less important than feeling comfortable. The key to special-occasion dressing—and we include vacations in the category of special occasions—is striking the balance between comfort and appropriateness.

Things would be so much easier if new categories of dress were not always popping up on invitations. What would King Frederick have made of "California Casual"? We'll never know, but we can help you parse out what your host or hostess has in mind. The first question to ask while parsing is: Why a dress code? Assuming your host and hostess are not sadists just dying to see you try and look good in "Hoedown Elegant," it is a way to foster a certain atmosphere. We once attended an afternoon wedding in Southern California that requested "Picnic Attire." We sat under beautiful umbrellas and the wedding lunch was packed into picnic baskets, complete with antique linens. It was a warm afternoon, and being able to laze about in clothing more casual than one might expect at a wedding—sundresses on women and khakis on men—gave the whole day an air of summery *dolce far niente*. The dress code went a long way toward creating the type of relaxed atmosphere the bride and groom wanted.

The ambiguity arrives when your feeling for what would further a certain atmosphere clashes with the host's. Certainly the most efficient way to solve this dilemma is by calling the host or hostess and inquiring what exactly "F. Scott Fitzgerald–Inspired" means. Sometimes you can't get a straight answer, either because the hostess thinks she is doing you a favor by not pressuring you—of course she's not because we'd all prefer to know exactly what is expected of us—or you have no means of contacting the host or hostess. In this case, you must do as much detective work as you can. Where is the event being held? What type of space is it? If the party is at the Pierre Hotel, that gives you one idea; if it's at the Brooklyn Brewery, that's another. Are the hosts stuffy lawyer-types or happening book editors? What percentage of the guest list will be tattooed?

Perhaps the most troubling of the newer common categories is "Festive Attire." We once attended a party where an elegant friend fulfilled the hostess's request by wearing his usual dark Armani suit with a string of illuminated Christmas lights draped around his neck. Although buying batteries for your wardrobe may not appeal to you, this solution offers an interesting lesson. No matter where you are going and what your host would like, you must remain true to yourself or you'll end up rushing out and buying something you'll never wear again. Plus, there is a good chance you'll feel uncomfortable in what you selected because it just isn't you, and you will be ill at ease as a result. That is something no host wants. This "to thine own self be true" idea of festive attire does not mean that you should show up in shorts, but it does mean that a bit of whimsy is almost always appropriate. Everyone likes whimsy! Back to the "Festive Attire" situation: This would be the moment to break out something sparkly. Not a Nolan Miller bead-encrusted gown, but a sparkly accent. Whimsical, sparkly accessories are ideal. This is a chance to tap into your inner Isabella Blow. We believe that festive calls for fun as opposed to super-sexy, i.e., eye-popping displays of cleavage. To many young women, it isn't going out if their breasts aren't hoisted to attention. There is something grimly predictable about such displays of cleavage. And this is true for any occasion. Why not highlight another part of you with some gorgeous, no-holds-barred shoes?

Or, if there is no way anybody is talking you out of wearing your favorite black dress and pumps, add a ridiculously huge cocktail ring and some red lipstick. Come on, live a little!

VARIATIONS OF BLACK TIE: OPTIONAL, ENCOURAGED, AND CREATIVE

These directives speak much more to men. Briefly, they can be interpreted thusly:

Black Tie Optional allows for a dark suit, white shirt, and dressy tie if you do not have a tuxedo.

Black Tie Encouraged is a way to strongly suggest that a tux be worn without making those who do not own tuxes feel inadequate.

Creative Black Tie is simply an excuse to wear a fresher incarnation of the tux—a black shirt or different type of tie, perhaps. For many men it might be simpler to keep the *conversation* creative and opt for classic black tie.

For women, all of the variations mean one thing: You have many options. It has been our experience that black tie is increasingly looking like "dressy cocktail" for women. In other words, dresses no longer must reach the floor.

Depending on how often you attend the types of events that call for black tie or one of its relatives, you may be better off with a fabulous—read: black—cocktail dress that can be "garnished" with beautiful accessories. If you are forever being called upon to attend balls, galas, and super-posh dinner dances, you may need to invest in a few floor sweepers. The gentlemen at the Consulate, as you've probably noticed, will be in white tie. This is the dressiest of all and requires black tails with a white shirt and white vest.

OFFICE PARTY

The issue here is how to strike a balance between the fun and the professional.

If the party is directly after work, this may be a moot point—you will simply wear whatever you chose from your well-organized closet that morning. Perhaps a quick mini toilette at your desk—if you have some privacy; if not, the ladies' room will suffice—to create a transition from work to socializing. Location is also key—if it's in your conference room with boxed wine, you probably don't need to dress—if it's at the Rainbow Room, tuxedo pants and a gorgeous shell might be the way to go. You are no longer at work but you are still with your coworkers. So again, restraint regarding cleavage is suggested. And restraint with the boxed wine and holiday punch is a wise idea, too.

CALIFORNIA CASUAL

This is a relative of the Florida Casual, Caribbean Casual, and Texas Casual. No doubt someone somewhere is planning a Minnesota Casual party at this very moment. California Casual does not mean wearing a T-shirt at the World Economic Forum in Davos, Switzerland, as Google cofounder Sergey Brin did. But rather this is a way to be polished but comfortable. This could mean a sundress instead of a cocktail dress. Or in the Texan case, cowboy boots instead of pumps. This is a modern incarnation of resortwear accessible to all of us, not just those of us wintering on Turks and Caicos.

DRESSY WARMTH

Men have very little to worry about when dressing up in the winter. A tuxedo is positively toasty compared to a strapless, décolleté-baring gown, so how do you look chic while not freezing? Some might say, "I'd rather freeze than wear a coat—one night of risking hypothermia is worth it!" While we admire the fashion *über alles* attitude, the problem remains that you will look unfinished arriving at your destination with chattering teeth and blue lips.

There are a few options that will always work. One, the cashmere, or cashmere-esque, stole. As we mentioned in the accessories chapter, the stole should be of an appropriate dimension for your figure and of a luxurious enough weight that it will provide some warmth and not look skimpy. Another option, which is less expected these days, is a faux-fur chubby. What an entertaining name for a style of jacket! Its only competition in the coat-name sweepstakes might be the balmacaan—a loose, swingy coat with raglan sleeves. You could also wear a balmacaan in a dressy fabric, but first, back to the faux-fur chubby. As the name implies, the chubby is a cropped, full, and fluffy fur hitting just above the natural waist. Our preference is for faux fur, since there are so many wonderful versions available today. Plus you could have a chubby *and* cashmere stole for less than you'd pay for a real fur.

One huge benefit of the stole and chubby is that they are short—therefore you do not have to worry about the length of your dress versus the length of your coat. Everyone is bit more relaxed today about hems peeking out from beneath coats, but sometimes, call us stuffy, it just doesn't look right. Why not opt for a warm outerlayer that will work with any length? Having said that, there are a few lengths that may not be ideal with a chubby. Something in the baby doll vein could be tricky. Since you obviously have some flair if you own a formal baby doll dress, how about a trench?

The trench coat for evening is a look we love. It's a very insouciant, "just threw this on over my Worth gown" look. Opt for a trench in black, especially in a fabric with some sheen, and you'll have a go-anywhere evening coat that will also work during the day. Again, be aware of competing hem lengths.

We now live in a time when it is possible to own a beautiful, chic—dare we say dressy—parka. Many designers have created what can only be described as evening puffy coats. We've even seen shirred mink varieties! These coats, if they have a dramatic collar, a nipped-in waist, or a beautiful rich color, do not look totally out of place when going out. Of course, put them on over anything more formal than a cocktail dress and you'll be on thin ice. But at least you'll be warm!

MEETING THE FAMILY

There are many occasions when one does not want to hide one's light under a bushel as much as make sure the light will be appropriately appreciated no matter what the venue. Although the above sub-heading suggests meeting a paramour's family, we think of it as any time you're the newcomer meeting a large, already established group. Confidence is essential in this situation. Upon reflection, when isn't it? However, meeting your new in-laws, medical practice partners, or fellow chess club members, you'll want to play it close to the vest. You'll know all about each other soon enough. Weather permitting, a wool jersey dress would be an excellent choice. The fabric has enough movement to be interesting, while avoiding fussiness. Furthermore, you'll be able to breathe, so if you must nip off to the bathroom for a little hyperventilating, at least only your nerves will be attacking you, not your clothing.

ROYAL WEDDING

When you get the invite, e-mail us. We will respond.

NON-ROYAL WEDDING

Weddings inject a bit of pomp and circumstance into our otherwise—we're speaking for ourselves—pomp-free lives. It should be an unabashedly happy occasion, so why not have some fun while putting together an outfit? Unless the couple is conservative, black is now considered fine, especially at evening weddings. A little research will be necessary if the ceremony is not one you are familiar with culturally. A small bit of Googling should reveal if it is terrible manners to wear pink to a Croatian wedding. If you do opt for black, add accessories in an unexpected color to lighten up the look. One thing that hasn't changed when it comes to nuptial fashion is the prohibition on white for guests. Frankly, white doesn't do that much for so many people, why not let the bride be the only one who has to wrestle with it on her special day?

Another rule, which is as old as the hills, mandates that shoulders should be covered during the ceremony. One can argue that this is only really necessary if the ceremony is taking place in a religious setting. However, why rob yourself of the big reveal at the reception? You'll whip off your wrap and stun the room with the beauty of your shoulders.

FUNERALS

We hope that in your life you attend far more weddings than funerals. Although black is still the color most closely associated with mourning, it is permissible to wear other dark colors. The focus should be on the proceedings, not your outfit, so opt for simple, conservative clothing.

PACKING

For some, packing is as stressful as death, divorce, or moving. But at least you can wear bright colors! Even business travelers can develop packing anxiety—but generally those frequent flyers have the right idea. You only need a couple of choices. Business travelers pare down their travel wardrobes and realize they only need two suits, an outfit for a dinner without the clients, and their running clothes. We should all be able to pack like this for everything. But that's no fun! Packing is serious business. As a way to add a bit of fun, may we suggest picking a narrative? Having a narrative is a way to streamline what you are going to bring. If you are going for "Urban Sophisticate Visits the South of France" you will not bring your "Hoedown Elegant" outfits as well. It is a theme around which to pack, a way to ensure that nothing makes it into the suitcase that shouldn't. You may be tempted by the packing theme of "Person Who Wears All the Things in My Closet That I Never Wear." Resist this. If that kimono top doesn't feel right in Berkeley, it won't feel right in Berlin, either.

The packing theme is also a way to avoid that malady that strikes so many travelers: Aspirational Packing Syndrome. Who knows, we might be invited to that dinner dance at the Albanian Consulate or pressed into last-minute service as an emcee at a silent auction while visiting family in Seattle. However, one of the wonderful things about being human is the unpredictable nature of life for which nobody can adequately prepare. The best-packed blouses of mice and men . . . If the Albanians simply demand you stop by, you'll just have to do some emergency shopping. Perhaps they will also demand you visit the salon of a famous Albanian caftan maker. Lord knows, an absolutely huge part of doing "Tirana Casual" is finding the perfect caftan.

So, back to packing: The good packer is able to look inside herself and be honest about what will be worn. We know, deep down, how many pairs of jeans we are likely to actually wear in a five-day period while visiting our parents for Thanksgiving.

Here is an exercise—just bring a carry-on. Make it a low-stakes trip, like the aforementioned Thanksgiving visit. Visits to family are often high-stakes emotionally, of course, but the dress code is often a bit more casual. Just bring what you absolutely need. No extra choices, no "just in case" or "I'm not sure what I'll be in the mood for" sweaters. Decide right now what you will be in the mood for, and then put it in your rolling bag. The idea of deciding what you will be in the mood for a week from Thursday may seem daunting; this is why a trip home is an excellent time to experiment. The terrain, both sartorial and emotional, is familiar. The types of outings you'll take, the level of formality, the fact that your mother wishes you'd wear more blush—you know it all going in, so you can wean yourself from those overstuffed bags with a minimum of apprehension.

UN VOYAGE IMAGINAIRE

To borrow a word from our favorite TV chef, Alton Brown, there should be no uni-taskers in your suitcase.

Let's put this principle to work on an imaginary trip to one of the most charming cities in the world: Montreal. You'll be going for three days and staying at a hotel right off Boulevard Saint-Laurent. Lucky you! First, pack two pairs of pants; both should work for day and night. Now add some shoes comfortable enough for sightseeing, but chic enough for dinner—may we suggest, yet again, the ballet flat? (Especially one of those new-fangled pairs that have sneaker technology.) Your handbag should be roomy enough for your digital camera and for the wonderful bagels you'll want to bring home. It should not, under any circumstances, be a backpack. Your trousers, which looked trim and chic while sightseeing, with the addition of a different top will stand you in good stead at the small-plate restaurant and bar in a converted warehouse right by the St. Lawrence River. After an evening out, you return to the hotel and slip into your preferred version of pajamas. Do bring an extra pair of socks or travel slippers. So three days can be handled with two pants, two tops that can go to dinner and three tops for daytime, a pair of ballet flats, some travel slippers, and sundry underthings. A cardigan sweater and a trench coat would round out the collection nicely.

Your efficient packing will leave plenty of room for the lovely mid-century items you pick up at Couleurs on St. Denis Street. And those bagels. That's what travel is all about, isn't it? You may regret not buying that incredible clock, but the chance that, months later, you'll rue not bringing that extra dress is minuscule. Lest you become too excited by all that space in your suitcase and fill it up with treasure, remember what the great decorator Albert Hadley once said, "Nothing has ruined more interiors than travel." As always, shop with discretion.

For those folk lucky enough to take tropical vacations, let us turn to those beach bags. Really, few voyages lend themselves to minimal packing like this one. This is a chance to free yourself from the tyranny of clothing. By day, all you need are swimsuits and tasteful cover-ups for lunchtime. The tasteful cover-up can be a sarong or pareo worn either as a skirt or dress. Another option is a *kurta*—an Indian top resembling a tunic, which will look equally chic over a camisole and jeans for the flight. The *kurta* also works at dinner with linen pants. Those *kurtas* are hard-working cover-ups! Tasteful cover-ups do not include mesh or anything that reveals more than it hides. Swimsuits are an entirely different thing. If you would like to have a different swimsuit for every day, go ahead. They are small and do take awhile to dry. Sandals with a little detail work for all aspects of this vacation—poolside, beachside, in town, at dinner, riding your moped . . . really, when are they not a good choice? We'll tell you: hiking. We trust that if you are the type of person who enjoys hiking on vacation, you know to bring something a bit more substantial.

The Blind Spot: Never assume. Going to Sorrento in April? Thinking that you won't need a light jacket? Hah! Before you leave home you *must* avail yourself of all the technology available today and check those temperatures! Although you cannot anticipate every meteorological exigency, a small amount of research will go a tremendous distance toward ensuring a happy trip.

Likewise, make that call to the host or hostess to inquire about the preferred dress. Just don't make it the day of the party. This should always be done if the invitation is communicated to you by a man. Not all men are guilty of this, but we've known a few who tell their date it's just a little get-together and it turns out to be his boss's cocktail-attire wedding reception. The poor things can't help themselves. Forewarned is forearmed.

Chapter Ten

Appendices

Style, as we may have mentioned, is about who you are. Since who we are shifts over time, our style stories are a never-ending bildungsroman. The secret to keeping your style story hop, hop, hopping along is to be forever expanding your cultural horizons. Since style is ineluctably related to the culture in which you live, the more you see, read, sniff, hear, or eat, the richer your engagement with the world around you becomes.

So perhaps the real secret to style is filling yourself to the absolute brim with engagement. Loving not wisely, but too well and all that. We thank you for sharing this time with us. We hope you find yourself returning to the book again, if only for a mere booster shot of the edicts of quality, taste, and style.

Our appendices offer a quick fix, as it were, to those edicts. We suggest that you use the following material and suggestions for investigation and research. These references have made us more fashion savvy, so why shouldn't they work for you? Here are some very brief suggestions to get you started.

FILMS OF STYLE

We are not recommending these films solely for their wardrobes—even though many of them are exemplary. These are films that will give your eyes a workout, either because of their breathtaking cinematography or because there is nothing like watching Cary Grant and Myrna Loy for two hours. Get that Netflix queue ready!

Blow-Up

Doctor Zhivago

The Women

Auntie Mame

Dark Victory

Persona

The Bachelor and the Bobby-Soxer

The Palm Beach Story

The Fountainhead

Funny Face

Dinner at Eight

The Philadelphia Story

All About Eve

Austin Powers

Sleeper

L'Avventura

Valley of the Dolls

The Devil Wears Prada

Infamous

Metropolitan

The Draughtsman's Contract

The Go-Between

Prospero's Books

Grey Gardens

Mildred Pierce

Last Year at Marienbad

Masculin Feminin

Funny Girl

Shampoo

Desk Set

A Place in the Sun

Cleopatra

BOOKS OF STYLE

This is a category of such immensity that we are loath to offer titles. Here is why: In the hours that we discussed which should be included, the list grew to more than 100 titles. If Toltsoy is on there, which he must be, than Dostoyevsky should be, too, because *Notes from Underground* has that whole overcoat thing and the narrator's grimy dressing gown, and what about Thomas Mann and Balzac and Rebecca West and . . . you see the problem. There is only one rule when it comes to books of style: If it makes you think about who you are and the world you live in, it will add to the reservoir of ideas and experiences that make you who you are and may influence the style choices you make. We therefore urge you to never, ever pass a bookstore without going in and doing as thorough a browse as time allows.

SCENTS OF STYLE

How one wants to smell is an extremely personal choice. In fact, you may have already decided that you want to smell like Jean Patou's 1000 for the rest of your life. Be that as it may, do not rob yourself of the opportunity to further educate your nose. It will only deepen your enjoyment of food, wine, chocolate, your partner, and anything you really love. In reference to the section above, have you ever noticed the distinctive smell of the pages of a brand-new hardcover book? Or the rapturous perfume of fresh lilacs? So, even if you are not interested in perfume for your person, do not ignore the olfactory!

If you are interested in perfuming your person, may we recommend a store to visit next time you find yourself in New York City? Aedes de Venustas at number 9 Christopher Street. The store itself is a visual feast and the range of perfumes contained within will provide an incredible education for the nose.

THE GLOSSARY

Few activities are as delightful as learning new vocabulary. With each newly acquired word comes the ability to articulate an idea with more elegance and precision. Learning the correct names and definitions for styles and textiles will not only allow you to articulate what you like, it will provide new insight into history, geography, and sociology. You may not personally need a rear furbelow—otherwise known as a false rump—but how can you not be intrigued by the cultural forces that gave rise to it? For a truly comprehensive guide, we recommend *The Fairchild Dictionary of Fashion*. Not only will it settle any arguments about what can or cannot be called a dolman sleeve, it provides hours of interesting browsing.

Here are a few terms we've used throughout the book along with some others, just for fun:

alpaca
Cousin of the camel, alpaca fleece is spun into a soft shiny yarn. Often combined with other fibers, alpaca is commonly used in sweaters, coats, and wraps. Similar to mohair. Alpacas themselves are social creatures with charming little faces, if one likes ungulates.

astrakhan

A pile fabric woven to mimic Persian lamb. Originally, the curly fleece of astrakhan sheep was used.

babushka

A square scarf folded to form a triangle. Worn over the head and tied underneath the chin. Best left to our elders who miss the Old Country.

bateau

From the French for "boat," this neckline is also referred to as a boat-neck. It is slit all the way to the shoulders while remaining high on the neck, both front and back. Quite graceful and feminine.

batik

A wax-resist dying method from Indonesia. The desired pattern is traced on fabric with wax and then dyed. The wax is removed to reveal the pattern, which has remained the original color of the fabric.

batiste

Soft, lightweight, and delicate cotton with a lovely hand. See *hand*.

batwing

An extremely close cousin of the dolman sleeve, this sleeve is also tight at the wrist with deepset armholes.

blouson
A look that involves a flowing top cinched below the waist. Currently enjoying a revival as a top worn with jeans.

box pleat
A one-way ticket to Frumpsville if not handled with discretion. A box pleat is an inverted pleat with a large "box" on either side of it. If confused, keep an eye peeled for schoolchildren in uniform; the girls' skirts will probably be box pleated.

braid
Used as a trim, often on coats.

burnt-out
This is a technique that employs chemicals to dissolve part of a textile, leaving behind a pattern. Often used on velvet.

calico
A favorite of the *Little House on the Prairie* set, this is a cotton fabric printed on one side.

camel hair
As you no doubt guessed, a warm and soft yarn from the hair of the camel. Makes a wonderful coat.

capri pants
Fitted pants that end between knee and ankle. Not to be confused with their looser sibling, the pedal pusher.

cashmere

Those poor ungulates, never a moment's peace! Yet another luxurious yarn that comes from a four-legged creature, in this case a goat. Soft and warm, cashmere is king of the knits.

challis

Sheer wool fabric often printed with floral designs.

charmeuse ·

A silky fabric with a crepe back, charmeuse can be made with a variety of fabrics, i.e., silk charmeuse. It is very difficult to work with, as every mistake shows, much to the chagrin of many beginning sewers.

chiffon

An almost transparent fabric known for its lightness and ability to drape.

cloche

From the French for "bell," this hat fits close to the head and has a tiny brim. Closely associated with the looks of the '20s.

corduroy

A heavier fabric distinguished by its wales, which vary in size from quite subtle and close together (pinwhale) to far apart and very noticeable (wide wale).

cotton duck
A heavy cotton fabric that, depending on weight, can be used for clothing, sails, or upholstery.

cowl neck
A draped, soft neckline that hangs in folds. Can be shallow or deep.

dart
A V-shaped tuck that allows fabric to form itself to the body. Well-placed darts are an essential part of a well-constructed garment. When trying a garment on, check to make sure that the dart placement works for your figure. In other words, if the dart that is supposed to give shape to the bustline hits somewhere around your collarbone, it doesn't fit.

deshabille
Literally, this refers to being only partially dressed. In fashion terms, it refers to a peignor or negligee, something one might wear while swanning around the boudoir.

dirndl
A style of dress associated with parts of Germany and Austria. The dirndl has a tight bodice and full skirt. A blouse is worn underneath the bodice.

dolman sleeve
Fitted at the wrist with extremely deep armholes. In a dolman sweater, it might almost appear that you were wearing a poncho—that's how wide the sleeves are.

doupioni

A silk fabric made from an uneven yarn that produces slubs in the fabric. Slubs are little bumps that give the fabric a textured appearance. Not the most attractive word, but a great look.

empire

A neckline or sillouette in which the waistline is directly under the bust, falling straight from there.

epaulet

An ornamental piece of fabric on the shoulder, most often on coats, but popping up on all manner of tops occasionally. Think of those shoulder items on a military trenchcoat and you'll know what an epaulet is.

flannel

A lightly napped fabric with a soft, somewhat cozy hand. Excellent, excellent for trousers, especially in gray.

French cuff

A shirt cuff that folds back—doubles—and is often fastened with a cuff link. Be you man or woman, keep the cuff link subtle. Otherwise the look gets very Gordon Gecko.

frog closures

If you've ever had any Chinese clothing, you've probably dealt with a frog. They are comprised of a corded loop and a large knot; slip the knot through the loop and you're closed.

gabardine
Available in both cotton and wool varieties, gabardine is a tightly woven fabric that is often made into pants and coats. The cotton variety is often used for trenchcoats.

gauchos
A split-skirt–style pant that should only be worn on the Pampas.

grain
The direction of the threads in a piece of fabric.

gray glen plaid
Wool fabric with a pattern of intersecting lines that form squares.

hand
Literally, how the fabric feels to your hand. Cashmere has a soft hand; burlap a rough one.

jersey
Not just a fabric, it's a whole classification. Silk jersey, wool jersey, rayon jersey, the list goes on and on. What they have in common is the fact that they are a knit without a rib: that means they are smooth and usually drape well. A fabric that Chanel did wonders with and still a staple.

jodphur

Riding pant that balloons at the thigh and then narrows. A tough look to pull off between the thigh ballooning and the fact that ones needs a horse nearby to not look like she is in costume.

lawn

A delicate, soft cotton that works beautifully in summer dresses and blouses.

le smoking

Yves Saint Laurent's blockbuster 1966 tuxedo suit for women. Originally shown with a frilly white blouse and black ribbon around the neck. Still fabulous.

linen

A fabric that comes from the flax plant. There is nothing cooler in the heat of summer and the fact that it wrinkles like crazy is just part of its charm.

maillot

A one-piece swimsuit, often cut low in back.

melton

A heavy fabric used for coats. Often a combination of wool and other fibers. Melton can be rough and is best for utilitarian purposes.

merino wool

A high-quality wool yarn that comes from merino sheep.

minaudière

A small, hard case carried as an evening bag. Judith Leiber is famous for her extremely sparkly versions.

mohair

Hair from the angora goat, used for everything from sweaters and coats to upholstery. Can be a bit prickly, so often works well in a blend.

muslin

Cotton fabric used primarily for prototyping garments.

passmenterie

Trimmings, like braid or cord. A lovely word.

peplum

A bodice that flares below the waist. One often sees peplum jackets.

Peter Pan collar

A small, rounded collar that rests flat. Although it occasionally pops up on womenswear, this collar is most closely associated with childrenswear.

pile

Yarns that stand up create pile. The yarns can remain uncut or be cut to various lengths. Terry cloth is an example of an uncut yarn.

pinked

An edge cut with pinking shears to prevent unraveling. The shears do not leave a straight line like standard scissors; instead they produce a saw-tooth effect.

piqué

A durable cotton with a raised, woven design.

princess silhouette

Tight through the bodice and waistline, full of skirt. What puts the princess in the princess silhouette is the absence of a seam at the waistline.

raffia

A palm fiber often woven to create hats or a decorative trim.

sack

Merci, Monsieur Givenchy, for the sack dress. He made the look famous and it is exactly what it sounds like. A dress with no waistline that hangs straight from the shoulders. *Über* chic in the summer with a pair of flat leather sandals.

seersucker

A puckered, striped cotton fabric associated with southern dandies and their white-shoe–wearing brethren. A lovely, classic material for summer wear. That means Labor Day arrives, off goes the seersucker.

self belt

Any belt made of the same fabric as the garment it comes with. You are not wedded to the self belt, and can always wear something else if you wish.

set–in sleeve

A sleeve sewn into the armhole. A kimono does not have a set–in sleeve.

sheath

The sheath has meant slightly different things over the years, but generally speaking, it is a fitted dress that gets its shape from darts.

surplice

A loose, draping neckline of two pieces of fabric that cross one another. The result is a soft V-neck.

trapeze

A look popularized by Dior in the late fifties and which is still with us. Think triangle: fitted through the shoulders, loose at the waist, and continuing to a full bottom.

vicuña

Ah, our final ungulate! Vicuñas are a type of llama that has exceedingly soft hair. A vicuña coat plays a small but important role in the Billy Wilder classic *Sunset Boulevard*.

We would like to thank Tamar Brazis and Susan Van Metre, our editors at Harry N. Abrams. Without their patience, fortitude, and whip-cracking, this book would never have been delivered—or at least not for many more months!

Tim would like to thank his mother, Nancy, who is the source of more than enough anecdotes for this book . . . and many others to come.

Kate would like to thank Tim for being the dearest friend and mentor one could ever hope for. She would also like to thank her darling Alex for all his generosity and love.

Tim Gunn is one of the stars of the hit Bravo show in which aspiring fashion designers compete for a runway debut at New York's Fashion Week. He is also the Chair of the Fashion Design Department at Parsons The New School for Design. He lives in New York City.

Kate Moloney is the Assistant Chair of the Fashion Design Department at Parsons The New School for Design. She lives in Brooklyn, New York.

ABRAMS IMAGE

This book was designed by Becky Terhune and art directed by Chad W. Beckerman and Mark LaRiviere. The illustrations are by Lainé Roundy. The main text is set in Bembo, an old-style serif typeface based upon one designed by Francesco Griffo in 1495. The version of Bembo used in this book is a revival designed by Stanley Morison for the Monotype Corporation in 1929. The display heads are set in Didot, designed by Adrian Frutiger in 1991 after the original by the French typeface designer Fermin Didot, and OPTILariatScript.